Tame Phone!

Controlling the tyranny of the telephone

■

POLLY BIRD

the Institute of Management

PITMAN PUBLISHING

The Institute of Management (IM) is at the forefront of management development and best management practice. The Institute embraces all levels of management from students to chief executives. It provides a unique portfolio of services for all managers, enabling them to develop skills and achieve management excellence. If you would like to hear more about the benefits of membership, please write to Department P, Institute of Management, Cottingham Road, Corby NN17 1TT. This series is commissioned by the Institute of Management Foundation.

To my parents, with love

PITMAN PUBLISHING
128 Long Acre, London WC2E 9AN

A Division of Longman Group UK Limited

© Polly Bird, 1994

First published in Great Britain 1994

British Library Cataloguing in Publication Data
A CIP catalogue record for this book can be obtained
from the British Library.

ISBN 0 273 60330 2 (Paperback)
ISBN 0 273 60690 5 (Cased)

Photoset in Linotron Century Schoolbook by
Northern Phototypesetting Co. Ltd., Bolton
Printed and bound in Great Britain
by Bell and Bain Ltd., Glasgow

Contents

■

iii

Acknowledgements

■

The Metropolitan Police Service, Division of Public Affairs, gave permission to reproduce the forms concerning bomb scares. Linda Phipps, Zack Goldring, Rory O'Kelly and Tessa Jowell MP, allowed me to quote them about telephone management. Mr B C Shadrach of Southwark Council talked to me about telephone training. The staff at BT and the Telecommunications and Posts Division of DTI were most helpful.

Particular thanks go to my agent, Teresa Chris, and to David Crosby and his colleagues at Pitman.

Last, but not least, I thank my husband Jon who always makes sure that I keep working!

Polly Bird, London, 1993

Introduction

∎

'Mr Watson, come here, I want you!'

When Alexander Graham Bell used these words to make the first phone call on 10 March 1876, he unleashed a power which has taken over every office. His assistant, Thomas A Watson, without the means to reply over the same line, was forced to answer the call by rushing over to Mr Bell. He started a trend which has continued ever since. When we hear the sound of the phone ringing we feel the need to answer it immediately.

Millions of business calls are made each day and every time the phone rings managers everywhere feel compelled to answer it. It disrupts their train of thought, forces them to reorganise their day and can make them feel powerful or powerless.

Like an unwelcome visitor it can irritate you, keep you from productive work, invade your space and drain your time. When answered it is an open door to letting unwelcome intruders in. With such a capacity for disruption and annoyance it is not surprising that the phone can be a major cause of stress, misunderstandings, complications and inefficiency.

It is a curious fact that this machine, which was designed to make life easier, has become the bully on the desk.

But it is not just the need to stop the ringing, or to find out who is calling, which make the phone such a powerful controlling force. How you respond to the person on the other end can make the difference to how the phone works for you. The fate of businesses large and small hangs on the ability to use the phone effectively. Your phone manner and how efficiently you use your phone for incoming and outgoing calls can make or break your business. A phone can be the greatest time-waster or the most powerful business tool. Which one depends on you.

Have you ever thought about how you answer the phone? Do you respond to everyone in a nervous way? Are you prepared for important calls? Can you get rid of time-wasters or do you let them ramble on? Do you control how calls are made and received during your working day?

My guess is, that like many people, you have just let your phone style evolve. You probably get by, but you could use your time more efficiently, pace your calls more effectively and control how you use your phone more usefully.

You may even be, like many people, nervous of using the phone. Do you let your secretary deal with important calls? Do you forget what you meant to say in the middle of that important conversation? But with careful preparation and improved personal phone skills you could change the efficiency of your working day for the better and keep callers under control.

Good phone technique will impress other busy managers with their own phone to tame. If you sound efficient and in control on the phone the reputation of your business will improve. At the same time a no non-sense attitude will deter time-wasters and unpleasant callers.

Any manager who feels bullied by the phone on his or her desk will find help in this book. It will take you through the basic strategies, techniques and advice needed to control the phone. By following these you could make a dramatic improvement in the way that the phone fits into your working day.

1

Who's boss?

We all think that we are in charge of our working day and that we could not possibly be bullied by the phone. But think carefully. How often have you picked up the phone today already? How many calls have you had to make?

Did the phone ring frequently throughout the day? Did it interrupt your work? Were many of the calls, both outgoing and incoming, unnecessary?

If you are honest with yourself you will agree that using the phone takes up too much of your working day. In addition, unwelcome or unnecessary calls irritate you and waste your time. You probably feel that you have to answer the phone whenever it rings. You think the calls you make are necessary and that you have to make them immediately – but is this really true?

You are not alone in your inability to use the phone efficiently. All over the world managers are asking themselves: why do I spend all my time on the phone and not get enough work done? How can I find time to manage when the phone demands so much of my attention?

If you want to keep your time free for more constructive work, you need to keep your phone in its right place. Ask yourself what you want to use your phone for. Do you want to:

- Relay important information quickly?
- Obtain information quickly?
- Pass on a request?
- Make an excuse?
- Discuss important work?
- Accept invitations?

All these are valid reasons for using a phone but only as long as the time taken to use it is in keeping with the importance of the call. This means that you will have to learn not only how to prioritise calls, but how to make calls efficiently. You are not always in charge of how you use the phone at the moment. You should be if you are going to work efficiently. Read on to see how to control the phone in your life.

This chapter will look at the pressure to answer the phone. It will show you how different types of people react to the phone and help you identify your own telephone personality. It will explain how to identify which callers you want to hear from and who you want to avoid. You will learn how to identify patterns in the calls you receive and make and what affected the calls.

By the time you have finished this chapter you will have clear idea of how and why your telephone bullies you and start to bring it under your control.

2

The tyranny of the phone

That technological marvel sitting on your desk controls you. It bullies you unmercifully and has no respect for your feelings. Don't let it get away with such autocratic tendencies.

There are many myths about using the phone. Let's dispel these straight away.

Myth: The more your phone rings, the busier you are.

Reality: The more the phone rings, the less time you have to get on with really important work. The chances are that most of your incoming calls can be dealt with by someone else, are from people you don't want to hear from, or go on too long. None of this means you are busy, simply that lots of people phone you – not the same thing. The effective manager keeps incoming calls to a minimum.

Myth: The more calls you make, the more important you are.

Reality: Why do you need to make a lot of phone calls? If you are that important you will have delegated the calls to someone else and reduced calls you have to make personally to a necessary few. Really important people are too busy with other things to spend all day on the phone.

Myth: The more you use the phone, the more sexually attractive you are.

Reality: We have all seen the films where the stars are busy executives who are constantly portrayed lounging in their chairs behind their desks with a phone in their hands concluding important deals while other phones clamour for their attention. This is supposed to be sexually attractive.

Be realistic: when does anybody except your colleagues see you on the phone? What makes you think you look sexy speaking into a machine instead of spending your undoubted charm on real people face to face? You will only be conveying an image of constantly chatting on the phone instead of the power image you want to convey.

Myth: The more phones on your desk, the higher your status.

Reality: Switchboard operators have the equivalent of dozens of phones in front of them and they don't run the company (oh, they run yours?). More than one phone means more time-wasters trying to reach you, less space on your desk for those important documents you have to deal with, and constant ringing noise.

3

Myth: The longer the phone call, the more informatio 1 it conveys.

Reality: You spent 20 minutes on the phone to Harry yesterday and discussed the football game, a dinner date, the state of the car park and, oh yes, you did mention that the proposal for CR Enterprises had to be in by Thursday. Long calls are rarely necessary, you must learn to cut them down.

Myth: The more calls you make and receive, the more business gets done.

Reality: See the previous myth. Also consider how much business actually gets finalised over the phone. Most of it needs paperwork and meetings. Phone calls are not useful for prolonged working out of business matters.

Myth: The office of the future is paperless, so I need to use the phone more.

Reality: *Your* office isn't paperless, and nobody else's is likely to be for a long time to come. In fact computers, faxes, etc, generate more paperwork than ever before. You need to get on with dealing with that before getting to the phone. Even in a paperless office you would need to cut down phone calls to work on your computer.

Recognise which of these myths you subscribe to and then jettison them. The time has come for you to crack the whip and get the upper hand over your phone.

THE PRESSURE TO ANSWER

Whenever the phone rings people feel the need to answer it. Try as they might they can't leave it ringing. This causes stress and all their work suffers. For example, the following situation probably sounds familiar.

You and five colleagues are having a business meeting. Half way through an important discussion the phone rings. You all pause. Does anyone say, 'Leave it, let's get on'? No. Everyone feels uncomfortable until somebody picks up the phone and answers it. The meeting is disrupted and your train of thought disturbed.

Some stress is good for you because it gets your adrenaline going and this helps you to cope with a challenge or to solve a difficult problem. But the stress of a constantly ringing phone is another matter and can lead to depression.

Part of the urge comes from the feeling that answering the phone is an important part of their job. It is true that using the phone is necessary in any managerial job nowadays but it is up to you how you use it.

Start now!

Later in this book I will show you in detail how to control how you use your phone, but for the moment try to curb your desire to pick up the handset immediately

First of all, think whether anyone will answer it if you leave it. Have you got a secretary? Then make sure that you allow time for your secretary to answer the call. That is what a secretary is there for. If you do not have a system of transferring calls between your secretary's phone and yours then leave it to ring for a few seconds before you decide that you need to respond.

Explain to your secretary that when the phone rings, you do not expect to answer it yourself. Your secretary should answer it and decide whether to pass the call to you.

Where you do have a call transfer system, use it and only ask your staff to switch calls directly to your phone when they leave the office. In that way you immediately cut down the number of times you need to answer the phone.

People often fear that a ringing phone means that the call is important or that there is something wrong. This especially occurs when the phone rings at an unexpected time, for example, just out of office hours. There is something about the idea of someone contacting you from a distance by means of the phone that plants the idea of importance or emergency into people's minds. They fear that if they do not answer it they may miss something important.

It is very unlikely that you will miss something important. If it is important the caller will phone back or fax you or speak to someone else in the organisation and ask them to get hold of you. If you have a secretary, the call will be answered and you will be informed about it. If you have colleagues who share the phone and you let them answer it they will tell you or leave a message.

If it is an emergency then it is likely that one of the emergency services is already dealing with the situation. If necessary, someone will call at your building to find you.

So do not be afraid about missing something important. Most phone calls are routine.

For some people it is the insistent sound of the phone that gives them the urge to answer it as quickly as possible. Sometimes it is so insistent that it makes people jump!

Do not let this overawe you. If you answer the phone immediately every time you will quickly become harassed. You need to train yourself be relaxed about answering a phone. If it is actually the loud ringing noise that worries you see if you can turn down the sound enough to reduce the raucous noise. Look for the volume switch on the side of your phone. But don't reduce the ringing so much that you can't hear it in a busy office. Let it ring five rings before you pick it up. You cannot let someone hold on the phone for very long before you answer it. Most training courses on telephone technique advise a maximum number of rings before you must pick the phone up and your organisation may have a client relations ruling which dictates how many rings you can leave.

In order to stop yourself responding automatically, let it ring the maximum number allowed. This will show you that the person on the

5

other end will still be there and that if you need to finish writing a couple of words or saying 'good-bye' to a colleague that you can do it without the phone exploding.

Train yourself to think of the phone as a useful tool under your control, not as a machine that orders you about.

THE PSYCHOLOGY OF THE PHONE

People react to telephones and making and receiving calls in different ways. Some people are confident users and treat the phone as simply another useful tool on their desk. Others are terrified of the machine and have to steel themselves to pick up the receiver to make or receive even the most basic of calls. You may see the phone as a power symbol or as a way of closer communication but most people, I'm sure, do not dream about a telephone.

It is important that you identify your feelings about the telephone and how you react to making and taking calls. Until you can sort out your feelings about it you will be unable to tackle the problem of how to control it.

Read the following descriptions of four common types of phone user. Try to work out which one most closely resembles yourself. Be honest and then you can start to deal with your phone.

Phone users fall into four distinct types:

- *Go-getters* – confident users
- *Shakers* – nervous users
- *Yes-people* – submissive users
- *Chatterers* – social callers

Go-getters

Go-getters are confident users who are not afraid of the phone. For them it is a useful machine which earns its keep in their busy life. These users are brisk and efficient and get straight to the point because they know what they want to say and what they want the phone call to achieve.

People who are confident on the phone can either use it efficiently, or badly. It is no good feeling happy about using the phone if you tend to ramble on or gabble. The truly confident user speaks clearly, keeps to the point, sounds cheerful and knows when to say good-bye.

The confident user who enjoys the phone as a social instrument has to curb his or her tendency to treat each call as an excuse for a chat. If you are a go-getter phone type then you must continue to be confident, but learn how to cut your calls down to the essentials and save the long conversations for home.

Go-getters keep calm before making any phone call and prepare for calls properly. They know that making calls when you are nervous or unsure of your facts will make you sound nervous and ill-prepared and will not inspire confidence in others.

Confident users practise at home by preparing for domestic calls and keeping to the point when talking to friends. They know the importance of making the most of training opportunities.

If you are not a go-getter learn to recognise confident callers on your phone. Listen to how they speak and how they use their time on the phone. When you have picked up tips from them you will earn their respect and be able to use that confidence towards other callers.

Reading this book will teach you how to prepare for calls and how to sound confident in your dealings on the phone.

Shakers

In contrast to go-getters, some people are scared of answering the phone. They trip over words, tend to gabble, forget what they want to say and usually prefer to write.

This can stem from many causes. Many people simply lack training about good phone usage. This means that they are simply unsure about how to use the phone properly. Even something as simple as what to say when you pick up the phone can make people nervous.

Other users think that they will not create a good impression on the phone. They forget that the caller cannot see them and talk as if the caller is in the same room and watching them critically. They ramble and choke on their words instead of sounding pleasant and cheerful. Clients find this a difficult person to do business with. They may feel equally nervous about talking to you!

Instead of speaking clearly and just slightly slower than usual their voices get higher with nerves. If you think you are a shaker then practise speaking like this into a tape recorder occasionally. You will be able to hear the difference.

Some people don't like making calls because they are afraid of disturbing the person at the other end. They forget that if they are phoning somebody in another office they are unlikely to get someone out of the bath! In a business situation everyone expects to get phone calls and so a call from you will not be seen as an interruption but a necessary part of business life. If the person you are calling is efficient they will have organised their day to take account of unexpected calls. So they will arrange for someone else to deal with you politely if you do call at an inconvenient moment – just as you should do in a similar situation.

Nervous phoners worry about not being able to see the other person's face. This can upset many people. We all like to be able to judge the response to what we say by watching the other person's face and judging their body language. The day of the video-phone on every desk, so that we see the other person on a screen, has not yet come. Lack of eye contact can be unnerving but again you can imagine it.

Are you simply nervous about the technology? Do machines scare you because you don't understand them and you are afraid they might go wrong? Even normally articulate people clam up when faced with a phone or microphone rather than a person. This is a well-known pheno-menon called 'microphone fright'.

This fright takes some people another way and they tend to talk ner-vously at the handset. An answering machine can make some people nervous because it is a disembodied voice. Some people don't like com-municating with a machine and they forget the message. They also worry about running out of time before the 'bleep'.

If you are a nervous telephone user, do not despair. There are techniques and tips to help you overcome your fear of the phone. This book will teach you how good preparation and some imaginative visualisation tech-niques will help to banish your fear of the phone.

Yes-people

Submissive phone users wonder if they've disturbed you, are apologetic and always agree with you. All you hear from their side of the conversation is 'Yes . . . yes . . . yes . . .'.

It can be very difficult to have a conversation with someone so submissive because you can never be sure that they really mean it when they agree with you. Getting a decision from them is hard work.

If you are like this then you must take yourself in hand. You will have to learn not to apologise for calling and to be confident that if your call is necessary then you must make it.

You will need to train yourself not to say yes to anything, unless you really mean it, if you find yourself saying 'yes' automatically. Good preparation and a clear knowledge of your aim in any call will help you do this and this book will tell you how.

If you are on the receiving end of yes-people, you will need to learn techniques for getting to the heart of what they really mean. Read this book to find out how to extract the most important information from a phone conversation.

9

Chatterers

Are you a member of this sociable tribe and like nothing better than to have a long discussion about anything other than the business in hand? Chatterers will expand their analysis of your recent report to include the weather, their outing to Manchester, their opinion of old Pete on floor seven and the general state of the economy. You need to cut them short and keep them to the point before you fall asleep over the phone or forget what it was you wanted to talk about.

If you are the chatterer then you have got to learn to keep your description of Annie's wedding to yourself until a more appropriate moment. Don't be like this common chatterer type:

'Hello, is that Simon?'

'Yes, how are you? Are you calling about the contract?'

'Yes. I've only just got round to it. I only got back from Annie's wedding yesterday. You didn't go to it did you? She looked lovely and of course Peter . . '

You will need to train yourself to prepare for your calls, incoming and outgoing, and to stick to the main point you want to discuss. You will need to be able to steer chatterers who phone you into a more relevant discussion of the business in hand. This book will help you do that.

A CAPTIVE AUDIENCE

Sometimes you feel that you are trapped into answering calls and that you have become a captive audience. You are captive if:

- there is nobody else at your desk to answer the phone
- there is nobody else in the office
- you are expected to answer a particular phone
- you have been asked to answer the phone
- it is your job (as receptionist, telephonist, secretary) to answer the phone.

There will usually be only one receiver on your desk, and unless you are connected to a three-way calling system, only you can hear the caller and reply. The moment you pick up the receiver you are a captive because you cannot leave the call without putting the receiver down. Only by replacing the receiver can you leave the room safely. If you leave the receiver off you have to return to it and the caller can hear anything people say at your end.

If you want to make a comment to someone else in the room you can press the mute button. This frees you from the knowledge that the caller is listening. Covering the receiver with your hand doesn't work. You can then release the mute button to finish the call.

Usually there is only one telephone line to connect the phone to each desk. This means that if you sit at the desk, you have to answer the phone and are the only audience available to the caller. You can free yourself by getting the calls transferred to somebody else or by leaving the answer machine on.

You can take pressure off by using a 'pickup' facility that enables anyone in an office to pick up any ringing phone. (Any one can pick up phones with single lines but only by physically moving to the other phone.)

FORCED PROMISES

Callers can be intimidating and you can feel bullied into making promises because you are nervous or unprepared. You can deal with this by anticipating callers. For instance, if you are expecting someone to call to discuss a proposal then you can anticipate that caller's wishes and what people are likely to ask you. You can have a set of answers prepared so that if you are caught on the hop you do not give an unconsidered reply.

If you still feel concerned do not give in but ask for time to think. Don't be pressured into giving a hasty answer which you might regret later.

Leave me alone

How do you get callers to leave you alone when you want them to (apart from keeping your answering machine on all the time with a message saying 'Do not phone me – I don't want to know')? You may want some calls because you need to discuss important business with the callers, but you can tame the rest by a process of organisation.

11

IDENTIFY PATTERNS

Get a large notebook and keep a telephone 'diary' for two weeks. Note down not only who calls you, but why and when. Add anything else about the caller that you think might be useful such as the firm, whether the caller frequently calls you, the attitude of the caller, how useful the call was and so on. For example, you might write Sally Noaks, re project list for FG Firm. Always calls on Friday morning before 10 am, very chatty, difficult to keep her to the point. Snaps if I disagree. When I get the information, it's usually helpful.

Questions you could ask yourself include:

- Was the caller helpful or time-wasting?
- Is the caller pleasant to talk to or rude?
- Is a chat with the caller usually useful or unnecessary?
- When does the caller usually phone?
- How do I feel after I have taken the call? Do I feel grateful, relieved, angry, afraid, nervous, pleased?

Do the same with calls you have to make. Was the call important? Did you have to make it at a certain time of day? How did you feel?

Use the log sheet illustrated as a guide to the sort of things you should put in your diary.

Call information diary					Date:	
Caller	**Company**	**Reason for call**	**Length of call in mins**	**Number and frequency of calls**	**Attitude of caller**	**Comments**
Betty Clark PA to CB	ABCD Fuels	To check on agenda for Tuesday's meeting with heads of department.	13 mins	Usually calls every Tuesday afternoon and once or twice on Fridays.	Aggressive and abrupt. Always criticises something about my work.	I dread Betty's calls. They make me feel nervous. I always feel upset afterwards. Her calls are usually unecessary or could be dealt with by her secretary.
Peter Sallis HOD – Energy	ABCD Fuels	To discuss my presentation to the conference next month.	12 mins	I usually speak to Peter about once a week – day varies.	Pleasant and keeps to the point. This was quite a long call for him.	I enjoy talking to Peter. We meet socially occasionally so we are on good terms.
Mrs Baker John's secretary	Carter Manufact-uring	Asked me to send John a copy of the tendering details.	2 mins	Once or twice a month. More often when rush orders on.	Brisk but cheerful.	Nice person and never wastes a call.
Ms D. Jones PR	Eagle Enter-prises	Read out press release for my confirmation.	7 mins	Once a fortnight or so. Usually on Weds. morning. Depends on what is newsworthy.	V. confident and plummy voice. Tends to gush.	Nice person but makes me feel inadequate. I enjoy talking to her but she tends to want a social chat.
My wife		Reminded me to phone Charles before I come home.	3 mins	About once a week – sometimes not for a month.	Usually a bit apologetic because she knows I prefer her not to phone me at work.	I try to tell her not to phone except in emergencies but she still likes to phone if she thinks I'll forget something.

Fig. 1.1 Example of a telephone diary

At the end of the period take a while in a quiet moment to look through your notes. You should be able to identify certain patterns in the calls. For instance, do you often get a lot of calls at particular times to the day? Does the same person phone you at particular times?

Are the calls from certain companies always time-wasting? Make a table of how long each call took so that you can see which calls were taking up most of your time.

Were the worst offenders your colleagues, outsiders, salespeople, or other types, e.g. a bomb hoax? What is your current response time and can you cut it down? Are you prepared for your calls or do they catch you unawares? Do you let callers ramble on or do you keep your phone conversations to the point?

Once you have an idea of your callers' patterns then you can organise them to reduce their calls so that you can make the most of your time.

IDENTIFY WORST INTRUDERS

First of all you need to discover who are the worst intruders into your working day by means of the phone. Look in your notes to find out who phones you most frequently. Is it someone from a particular company? Or someone from elsewhere in your firm? Make a note of who they are and when they usually call.

Then again, the intruder may be someone who always asks difficult questions. They may call without warning and ask you to find out something that would call for a lot of research and expect you to know the answer. Write their name down and the sort of questions they ask you.

IDENTIFY REGULAR TIME-WASTERS

By now you should have an idea of the categories of callers who upset your day. Another group to add to your list is the time-wasters. These are the callers who have nothing important or useful to say but just want a chat, or the person who finishes discussing business but rambles on because they don't know how to say good-bye, or the person who always wants to ask you silly questions.

You need to identify these people and cut them off quickly before they waste your time. Ideally you should stop them from calling you altogether. The next chapter will explain how to do this.

IDENTIFY REGULAR IRRITANTS

These are people who are perfectly polite and who always claim to have a good reason for calling but who manage to phone just a bit too often on minor matters.

It is difficult to avoid them because they phone so often and you cannot dismiss them if they say they need to talk to you.

When you have identified them from your phone diary make a point of saying to them 'I think we'll find that more will come to light on this subject during the week. Let's wait until we've got all the information and discuss it on Friday' (or whatever your preferred day is). That way you will avoid answering many short minor calls and eventually your irritating callers may get the message and save their calls up.

14

Ring me more often

Now that you have identified the callers from whom you don't want to hear and have seen whether there is a pattern to their calls (e.g. Frank from Accounts always phones on Thursday afternoon for a long chat) then you can work out from whom you *do* want to hear.

IDENTIFY WHO YOU ENJOY HEARING FROM

Who do you enjoy hearing from? Who keeps their calls short and to the point? Who asks if you are free to take the call? Who doesn't make you feel nervous? Who always phones with something useful to tell you?

Look at your notes and write the names of these people down with what they call about and when. Their pattern of calls is probably different to those whom you want to avoid. You can see at once that you can arrange your work so that you are working on something you can interrupt safely when the time-wasters call.

WHO IS GOOD ON THE PHONE

People you enjoy hearing from and who can be useful are usually good on the phone and know how to use one to best effect. Decide who knows how to handle a phone call and who tells you who they are and what they want straight away. Who makes sure everything is clear before ringing off?

These are the kind of calls you want to encourage. Like you these callers have their own work calls planned and will probably have their own pattern of calls. See how they fit in with your day. You should find it easy to arrange to hear from these people. Tell them when you would like to hear from them and they will try to accommodate you.

WHO USES PHONE CALLS TO YOU WELL

Good callers are effective on the phone and make you feel that the call has been worthwhile answering. Who knows what they want to discuss and gets on with it? Who makes sure they have everything clear before ringing off? Note these names as well because these are the people who are important to your working day and from whom you need to hear.

Calls you hate to make

Now that you have found out what the pattern of calls to you are you can start to plan your day around them and to use avoiding strategies if necessary. I will discuss how to do this in detail in Chapter 2.

Another problem about making sure that you are in charge of your phone is that you have to make calls out of your office. This may sound easy; after all, in those cases *you* decide when you pick the phone up and how the conversation will go. Or do you? Making calls can be just as stressful as receiving them and the kind of stress can be different each time you call, depending on the time of day or the mood you're in. You may, for example, always hate making morning calls because you do not relax until the afternoon or you may have to make an important call when you are starting to get a cold. Neither of these situations will make phoning somebody easy or pleasant.

IDENTIFY THE PROBLEM

You should be able to look at your phone 'diary' and see which calls you hated making and why. When you have to make a call and you hate doing it try to identify the problem. This could be one of a number of things or several or all of them. It may be that you dislike or fear the other person. For some reason they make you nervous; perhaps they have a brisk phone manner or are habitually rude. Maybe you simply dislike their way of talking and they are unclear or ramble on too long. It could be that you are nervous about the thought of interrupting them. Perhaps it is someone senior to you and that makes you worried. Whatever the reason it is the person themselves that worries you.

It could be the subject of the conversation ahead that concerns you. Perhaps you are not sure of the subject or have not had enough time to finish the research or write up a paper. Maybe you have to make a complaint about their service or tell somebody something unpleasant, for example that your firm will not deal with them any more because they have not paid their account. Maybe you are having to repeat a call because you forgot to ask all the necessary questions the first time. It could be that you have to make a request and are not certain that it will be well received. Whatever it is, preparation is the answer and this again is discussed fully later the book.

Some people are simply scared of the phone itself. It is a mechanical object and this worries them . It is impersonal and this means they can't relate to it properly. They may simply have a phone phobia or be struck with 'microphone fright' and be unable to talk to a machine. In this case they need training and the support of someone more confident in telephone use.

TIME AND MOOD

The reason for hating making certain calls is not always the same. When and how you make the call both play their part. Making a call last thing before going home when you are feeling tired may make the call unpleasant. See if you can work out when you hate making calls and why.

The time of day that you make a call can make all the difference to how you felt about making it. Are you a lark or an owl? Do you enjoy getting up early and getting on with your working day or are you half asleep until after the mid-morning break? If you are an owl person you may be too sleepy to concentrate early in the day. On the other hand you may miss an important deadline if you leave making your calls until too late.

16

If you worry that you may interrupt the other person find out when it is a good time to call and then call them back. If you have to call them regularly arrange for a mutually convenient time so that neither of you wastes your valuable working time.

Being in a good mood helps you to make calls because you feel confident and relaxed. You relay this happiness to the other person. Even if they can't see you, you will sound happier over the phone. Feeling good will also make you feel braver.

If you are in a bad mood you will feel scared. The other person will sense this and may take advantage of your nervousness. If you are unhappy you may not concentrate properly on the phone call. You are more likely to annoy or upset the other person by being cross. If you are feeling unhappy you might cry if the other person is cross with you and this will not make a good impression. Being upset yourself may mean that you are likely to misinterpret the other person's mood in the light of your own feelings. This will cause a lot of misunderstanding and may upset the other person.

One aspect of phoning someone when you are not feeling your best is that you may forget messages or to take notes or forget what you have promised to do. The answer is to try to make your calls when you are feeling well and in a good mood. Decide which calls are important and arrange to make them at a time when you feel at your best. If for some reason you cannot delay making them and you do not feel on top of things, explain this to the other person. Make sure you have your notes prepared and take notes as you talk. If you really can't face a particular call then just make a quick call to tell the other person that you will phone them at a later date. Try not to phone people when you cannot cope with it.

Call back crisis

Don't let all the return calls you have to make mount up until you have so many that you panic. If you cannot delegate the calls to someone else then a quick call back will save you from getting them stockpiled and will keep business moving. You can safely leave calls you can delegate to someone long as you have given clear instructions about what to say.

Summary

There are many myths about using the telephone: that using the phone a great deal means you are busier, more important, more sexually attractive, convey more information and have a higher status than other people. Most of these myths can be jettisoned. Overuse of the phone will not help you achieve more free time for other work or help you to be more efficient unless you use it only when necessary.

Before you can learn how to control your phone you need to identify which of the four main types of caller you are and learn to recognise these types of caller in other people. You may be a confident Go-getter, a nervous Shaker, a submissive Yes-person or a sociable Chatterer. Once you have identified your telephone type you can take steps with the help of this book to improve your telephone technique. You will also be able to deal better with calls when you know how to recognise these types of callers.

You may feel trapped into answering the telephone, but you can start immediately to take control of your phone. To get over the feeling of being trapped by the phone you must learn to identify which callers you want to hear from and those you do not want to answer. Keep a telephone diary. Make a note of who calls you when and how you react to them. Decide which calls you hate to make. After a few weeks you will be able to identify when you get your favourite calls and can prepare for the less welcome ones.

Make calls when the time and your mood makes you feel relaxed and confident.

By starting at once to work out how the phone fits into your day you can begin to make the pattern of phoning work for you.

18

CHECKLIST

1 Don't believe telephone myths.
2 Let the phone ring a few times before answering.
3 Identify your telephone type.
4 Don't become a captive audience.
5 Identify phone call patterns.

6 Keep a phone 'diary'.

7 Identify time-wasters.

8 Encourage callers from whom you want to hear.

9 Make important calls when you feel good.

10 Sound confident.

Incoming calls

The most difficult problem facing any manager who wants to create more time free from the phone is what to do about incoming calls. As you know, it is important that incoming calls *do* get answered, if not by you then somebody else. As Tom Peters said in *The Excellence Challenge*, 'The only magic of the $40 billion giant IBM is that in a $500 billion industry they happen to be the only company that answers the phone.'

To ensure that you and your company give the best service and are as productive as possible, somebody must answer each phone call. At the same time you need to get on with other things and cannot afford to spend all day answering the phone. So what are you to do?

You can exercise control over the calls you make yourself, but you cannot always anticipate who is going to call you and when. So how can you reduce incoming calls, or at least regulate when you answer them?

This chapter will show you how to schedule incoming calls to free your time. It will tell you how to anticipate and prepare for incoming calls so that you waste as little time as possible. It will tell you how to take effective messages and how to delegate answering the phone to other people.

By the end of the chapter you will be able to reduce your incoming calls to a minimum and answer most of them at a time convenient to you.

How to stop the ringing

When the phone rings you must resist the temptation to answer it yourself immediately. If you do, your days will always be punctuated by calls either from people whom you don't want to hear from, or from people you do want to listen to but who are calling at an inconvenient time.

As a busy manager you need to keep as much of your time free as possible for your work. The phone is a useful tool but you must not allow it to disrupt your working day. It must fit in with your work schedule; you should not need to bend your day to accommodate it. This is easier to do with calls you make yourself, but with incoming calls you must use other tactics.

DO NOT DISTURB

If you are in an office where colleagues pass calls to you then you must be firm. Say 'I'm busy this morning. I cannot accept any calls until after 2 pm' and then resolutely refuse to accept the phone if a colleague wants to pass it to you. It may not make you popular, but your work time will increase.

You can instruct people working for you in the same way. Tell them when they are not to disturb you and ask them to tell the caller either to phone back when you are free or to leave a message.

Anyone whom you ask to field calls on your behalf, whether your secretary or another, should be trained to take good messages. This is an art in itself and I will discuss it later in this chapter. Suffice it to say here that the messages should be detailed, clear and with all the *relevant* information in them. Make sure that everyone who works for you knows how to take a good message and has the necessary paper and pen to hand. Then let them do it.

One of the fears of some managers is that if they allow someone else to answer the phone for them they will miss out on something vital. Do not succumb to this. As a manager your job is to delegate as much as possible to competent people under you so that you have more time for the important work. If you have not got competent people then either change them or train them.

You will not miss something vital by delegating phone answering to someone who has been trained to take a good message. At the worst you can phone back to check in detail. At best you will have enough information to act without contacting the caller again. Either way, you will have freed yourself for some time from the chore of answering the phone.

21

You can schedule your calls, as I have mentioned. Apart from instructing those in your organisation that you cannot accept calls except at certain times, let your contacts outside the company know that they can only contact you by phone *personally* at certain times. If the caller is making a general call they will not need to talk to you in person anyway. If they need to talk to you they will call when they know you will be there. Try to have at least two times for accepting personal calls – one during the day and another outside normal office hours if possible, e.g. 8–9 am. This gives other busy managers a chance to schedule their day and increases their respect for you. By getting calls over at unusual times the day is more open.

DISCOURAGE TRANSFERS

One of the banes of office life is having calls passed to you because 'I didn't know who to put the call through to, so I chose you'.

22

You cannot allow this if you are to be in control of your working day. Tell the telephonists firmly that you will not accept calls unless they are specifically for you. If they don't know to whom to put the call through then they must find out and ring the caller back.

Do not accept internal calls that are passed to you without reason either. If there is no warning message of the 'Hello, Jane, I'm putting a call through. Can you deal with it – it certainly isn't our department' type then tell the caller that you are transferring the call back to the switchboard because it has been put through to the wrong place.

You may feel that this is impolite. Make sure that the switchboard operators or your secretary are equipped with a list of all departments and names of managers with brief details of their jobs. A check through the list should inform them who can most likely deal with the caller and so people are less likely to pass calls on at random.

Forewarned is forearmed

Knowing when you are likely to receive calls takes you halfway to being able to control incoming calls to suit *your* time schedule. This is not as impossible as it sounds because, if you think about it, you will already have some idea about when you expect certain people to call.

ANTICIPATING CALLS

You will already know that certain people are likely to phone at certain times. For example, Mrs George always phones on Thursday afternoon just after lunch because that is when she has to check the new orders with you, and Mr Green usually phones on a Monday morning because he has *his* time organised and wants to get his main phone calls out of the way early.

Take a few minutes to write down a list of all the people who regularly call at certain times. You may begin to see a pattern. For example, if you see that most of these calls come in the first half of the week try to ask the few 'stragglers' who call at the end of the week to call earlier, thus leaving the second half of the week relatively free from calls.

Sometimes you or your firm will have initiated calls and there will be situations when you can anticipate fairly accurately that your incoming calls will increase. For example, supposing you have just advertised, you will receive not only calls relating to your advertisement directly but also you will be inundated with calls from people wanting to sell you space in other publications.

If you have just written to someone requiring a reply, then it is possible that you may get the reply by phone. So you should be aware of this possibility.

23

PREPARE FOR INCOMING CALLS

Knowing that you are likely to receive certain calls or calls at certain times you can prepare for them. If you know that you will get a lot of calls asking for information about your product after you have advertised then you can prepare a standard response to save time, perhaps something like 'Thank you for calling. I'd be happy to send you some information if you give me your address or fax number'. Or, for example, to the advertising salespeople 'Thank you for calling. You will need to contact our sales department on extension 765'. An answering machine can come in very handy on these occasions. The use of these and other modern technological aids are discussed later in the book in more detail.

If you know that Mrs George will be phoning every week then you can have the necessary information for her to hand before her call and save a lot of time. Or you may know that *somebody* is likely to phone you during the next few days about the proposal you have just sent round. In that case keep the proposal and the answers to possible questions in your desk drawer so that you do not have to search for them or think up answers on the spot when the call comes.

If you have a secretary or another member of staff to take messages for you then alert them to the calls that you know are likely to come so that they are prepared. Agree with them a standard response to the expected types of calls and be specific about which calls you wish to have passed to you.

Anyone who takes a call, whether you or someone who is acting for you, needs to know how to take good messages. For instance, where you need information from anticipated callers you can prepare a series of questions which they can ask.

CALLERS WHO DON'T KNOW WHAT THEY WANT

Most of your callers will be people like yourself with a clear idea of what business they want to get on with over the phone. However, occasionally you will get callers who have not prepared for their call properly and who are not sure quite what they want from you. For example, your conversation may go like this:

Good morning. Is that Mr Jones?'

'Yes. Bob Jones speaking. How can I help you?'

'I'm phoning about the proposal. Gerry Marsh said I should contact you.'

'What in particular did you want to discuss?'

'Well, all of it I suppose. It has to be in on Monday morning.'

'But what aspect needs discussing?

'I'm not certain, but . . .'

In this case your task is to elicit as much information from them as possible so that you can judge what it is they really want to know. Try to get a clear understanding of what the caller wants before you go into detail:

'Good morning. Is that Mr Jones?'

'Yes. Bob Jones speaking. How may I help you?'

'I'm phoning about the proposal. Gerry Marsh said I should contact you.'

'What did Gerry Marsh want you to contact me about?'

'About the proposal.'

'Is that the proposal for new tenders or re-evaluation of company ordering systems?'

'The proposal about new tenders. I have to discuss it with you.'

'Yes, you do need to talk to me about it. Which part in particular? The pricing or the general policy?'

'The pricing . . '

Be careful about making assumptions too early. Don't start giving a reply until you are sure what the caller wants. To get the necessary information you need to:

(i) Ask questions. Don't be afraid of asking seemingly silly or obvious questions. The caller may know what he or she means but you do not until they have made it clear.

(ii) Repeat statements. If the caller says something vague, turn it into a definite statement and wait for a yes or no from the caller. When you get a yes then you are on the right track. Doing this will also clarify the caller's thoughts.

(iii) Don't make assumptions If the caller's thoughts are vague you may assume that he or she wants something other than what they really want. Use the repeating and questioning techniques above until you are sure you *know* what the caller wants.

The art of taking messages

Incoming calls do not cease because you are out of the office. In your absence you should arrange for somebody else to take phone messages for you. You, too, should develop your skills in message-taking. Business can be lost and reputations ruined if phone messages are recorded inaccurately or not passed on quickly to the person they are meant for.

Unfortunately, taking messages is not something that you can assume everybody can do with equal skill. An untrained person taking messages will often miss out something vital but obvious such as the date, time or even the name of the caller! And be honest with yourself, if you have to take a message for a colleague, do you note down *all* the relevant information and pass it on quickly? You cannot afford to ignore the art of taking messages and should ensure that all your staff understand the principles involved and practise them regularly.

KEY SKILLS IN MESSAGE-TAKING

There are certain key skills to taking messages which everyone who answers the phone should be aware of. They include:

- careful listening
- accurate note-taking
- sensible questioning.

Not everybody has these skills or exercises them. As it is your phone you are to control then you must make sure that everyone who might answer the phone for you, including yourself, has been trained in telephone message-taking.

The use of a phone message pad is discussed in more detail in Chapter 5, but the key skills are broader than just filling in a pre-printed form.

Naturally the pre-printed form which you will make sure everybody has will be a useful guide to what they should ask a caller. Insist that everybody fills in all the sections. Many people just do not look at a form properly or cannot be bothered to fill in all the sections. 'Does it really matter,' they think, 'if I don't fill in what time the call came?' You must impress upon everyone, and remind yourself, that every time a call comes in they must complete the phone pad in full.

Listening

Everyone who receives a phone call must listen carefully to what is being said. It is easy to make mistakes:

'Good afternoon. Is that Miss Bars?'

'Yes. What can I do for you?'

'It's about the new contract for Peterson's . . .'

'Peterson's? Are you sure you have the right department?'

'Yes. You are Miss Bars of the contract department?'

'No. I'm Ms Vase of the survey department.'

If the person answering the phone mishears a name or inaccurately interprets a message then it could cause embarrassment or worse for your organisation and call into question your own competence. If there is a general muzziness on the line then ask for a telephone engineer to check the line and installation for you to make sure that it is not a technical problem. If you or your secretary find it difficult to hear what callers say on the phone then you must get your hearing checked by a doctor. If necessary, ask for a loudspeaker phone which amplifies a caller's voice.

NOTE-TAKING

Accurate note-taking of calls is vital. If you are not sure that you have a spelling of a name correct then ask for your caller to repeat it or spell it out. Write all names of people or companies in capital letters. Double-check any figures or times. Write any message in full sentences and read it back to the caller to check its accuracy. Double-check that you have filled in all the details on the form before you let the caller ring off.

27

QUESTIONS

It is no good thinking that you will always understand what a caller means. If you are unclear about anything you must ask the caller for more information. In the case of anticipated calls you will have a checklist of questions you want to cover so make sure that you have asked all of them. Instruct your staff on the questions you want them to ask of certain callers.

There may be question that you want to ask all callers such as their address, which they may not all give automatically, or the name of the person who recommended your organisation. Either incorporate these into a message pad specifically geared to the needs of your firm or instruct everyone to ask the questions of every caller. You could pin vital questions on a telephone message board by every desk.

FURTHER ACTION

Encourage anyone who takes a message for you to take further action where possible. If the caller phones about something that the person taking the message can deal with, then this frees your time. Even if it is only checking on the contents of a file or finding out whether a course of action is possible this will save your time.

For example, you could get a message that says 'Mr Smith of Smith & Co. rang at 11.30 am. Please call him back on this number.' This may be an accurate message but it does not save you from having to make a call to Mr Smith to find out what he wanted and then to deal with whatever it is.

A far better message would be 'Mr Smith of Smith & Co. rang at 11.30 am. He wants to know if he can deliver the cartons before 9 am on Tuesday. I have established that Peter and Mike will both be in by 7.30 am but neither know the warehouse procedures. Please call Mr Smith back on this number.'

This saves you the trouble of finding out what you need to tell Mr Smith. You can then phone back briefly to say not 'Thank you for calling, Mr Smith. How may I help you?' but 'Thank you for calling, Mr Smith. We can deal with your cartons by 9 am on Tuesday. Please ask the deliverers to bring form A17A and sign the delivery book.' A quick call, to Mr Baker of the warehouse established that he can alter his schedule to supervise Peter and Mike.

This kind of enterprising reaction to message-taking not only saves you time but contributes to the efficiency of your organisation. You will also sound competent and efficient when you phone back and impress the client who will be more likely to use your firm again.

It will also encourage your staff to take more responsibility and make their life more interesting.

The art of delegation

This leads us neatly on to the art of delegation. I hope you are not one of those managers who thinks that only you are capable of making or answering phone calls or who can deal with all the calls that come in.

28

First of all, you simply haven't got time to hog the phone. You need to keep yourself free for more important work which is why you are in the position you are. Secondly, it is insulting to your staff and colleagues to assume that only you have the intelligence to use the phone.

If your staff do not take messages or respond to phone calls as you would wish then it is your responsibility to ensure that they are properly trained to do so – and once they are trained to encourage them to take more responsibility for calls.

People respond well to being given responsibility. Much work in an office is routine and anything which gives people the feeling of being useful and making a worthwhile contribution to the organisation is to be welcomed. Work becomes more enjoyable and efficiency increases. Not only will you have a happier staff but a more efficient office.

Once you have trained your staff then you must believe that they can often return calls as effectively as you can. In the example of Mr Smith quoted above, a manager who had trained his staff well might have encouraged the person who took the second message to call Mr Baker at the warehouse and then call back Mr Smith him or herself. If it is within the bounds of someone's capability and not wildly outside the sphere of their job then why not let them do it?

It is important that you encourage and praise anyone who does respond courteously, efficiently and responsibly to phone calls. If you encourage staff to take on more responsibility and get them to improve it is depressing for them if you then ignore their efforts. You can pat yourself on the back when you find you have less phone calls to respond to and more time for your work.

Do not be afraid that people who call and ask for you will think less of you if you do not reply to them in person. On the contrary, it will impress them that your firm is so well organised and has such helpful staff that they do not need to disturb you. It also implies, if you need to do so, that you are busy with very important work and cannot be disturbed. Of course you will instruct your staff about which calls must definitely be passed to you.

The old saying, 'First-rate managers pick first-rate staff; second-rate managers pick third-rate staff', can be applied to dealing with phone calls. First-class managers make sure their staff are all first-class at dealing with phone calls; second-rate managers let their staff continue to be third-rate at dealing with phone calls because they do not want to delegate responsibility to them and prefer to deal with all calls themselves. I hope you are going to be a first-rate manager about this.

Tessa Jowell MP, has no hesitation about relying on her PA to handle calls:

> *Most of the calls however go directly through to the office and Shelley [PA] will deal with the casework type calls and diary arrangements. Most of the others she will pass to me unless they are relatively straightforward requests for information, progress on an issue, etc.*

When you receive calls yourself, do not be afraid to pass them on to someone else if you can. Although passing calls on can be an effective technique for discouraging an unwanted caller (see the next chapter) for other calls you should be sure that the action is appropriate.

If the caller is not unwanted but merely inconvenient you could transfer the call to a colleague whom you know has the time and expertise to deal with it. Or you could ask the caller to phone later.

If you think that transferring a call is appropriate make sure that you manage the transfer politely and efficiently. Sighing deeply and saying, 'Listen, why not try Jones. He might be able to deal with you' will not go down well. Saying, 'The best person to talk to is Mr Jones. He has the paperwork about this and I know he will be able to help you. I'll just transfer you' is far better.

Whatever you do, do not simply transfer someone without saying anything. If you need to go through the switchboard then tell the caller that you are doing so. Give the name of the person you are transferring the call to and their extension number so that if for any reason the call goes astray or gets cut off the caller can redial and ask for the person you were transferring him to. By giving the other person's name the caller can ask 'Is that Mr Jones?' when put through.

Of course, you can also tell your now well-trained staff to transfer certain calls. Make sure they have a list of departments and staff areas of expertise so that they can get to the right person. For other calls you can say 'Unless it's Miss Fine or directly concerned with this department please will you transfer the caller to the relevant section.' Your staff can then use their judgement about where to transfer callers to. Do tell them not to transfer your spouse though – you might not find yourself popular when you get home!

Using your secretary

If you have a secretary then not only do you have someone who is in an ideal position to relieve you of your phone problem, but someone to whom you not only could but should be allocating more responsibility for it.

As with all members of your staff, you should ensure that your secretary is trained in good telephone technique. You should give clear instructions about whom you do and do not wish to speak to. You should also make sure that your secretary knows how to deal with unwanted calls and which kinds of calls to transfer.

Encourage responsibility for dealing with calls that are not urgent and those you do not need to deal with personally. This means encouraging the asking of questions to find out more about what the caller wants and giving your permission to act upon the information. Make it clear what you want done about callers whom they could deal with but who absolutely insist on talking to you personally.

31

If the caller is a major client this should be a straightforward decision – indeed you have probably already told your secretary to put through Mr Brown of New Account straight away whenever he calls – and of course your boss! For other callers that old white lie is useful – 'She's in a meeting – I don't know when she'll be out. I'll get her to call you later'. Without calling you or your secretary, there is nothing they can do about it but wait for a call from you at your convenience.

You should also instruct your secretary as to how you like your phone answered. It is very off-putting to phone senior members of an organisation and to hear a secretary's voice that just says 'Hello'. This happens surprisingly often and does not convey a good image of the organisation.

The caller is left wondering whether he has phoned the right organisation, let alone the right person! The correct reply is 'Seaweed Containers. Mr Jones' office'. The caller then knows that not only has he dialled the right number for the firm but that he has reached the right office. The secretary can then deal with the call according to your instructions. (Nobody should say 'Mr Jones' phone' unless they happen to be in someone's office and pick up the phone actually on Mr Jones' desk.)

Your secretary should sound pleasant. Many people are nervous about phoning and want to hear someone who sounds as if they will be helpful and not critical on the other end of the line. A good secretary, or indeed anyone answering a call, can make a caller go away feeling pleased even if he or she has not reached you.

Your secretary should be able to use common sense about when to say to you 'I've got Miss Adams on the line. Will you take the call?'. They will know that there are some callers you may need to talk to even if you are busy but that you may not be able to respond immediately. You can then say 'Yes, ask her to hold just a minute' or 'No. Apologise and say I'll call back in 20 minutes'. You can then rely on your secretary to take the appropriate action.

Managers want phone-competent secretaries. But do not allow secretaries to act as a guard dogs unless you are sure you can trust them to use their discretion sensibly. Although you want to reduce your incoming calls and control them, you don't want to find that you don't get any because your secretary tells everyone that 'He can't be disturbed at all today'! When well-trained in phone technique a good secretary can ease your phone problem a great deal and become a valuable ally in your fight to reclaim your time.

Summary

Anticipating and scheduling calls to a time convenient to you increases the time available for other work. It helps you plan your time and prepare effectively for calls.

Start by ensuring that you are not disturbed by the phone while you are doing other work. Do not pick up the phone immediately and refuse to accept calls except at certain times. Encourage your staff to answer the phone for you and discourage transferred calls.

Learn to anticipate incoming calls by being aware of who is likely to phone you and at what times. Your phone diary will help you with this. When you can anticipate calls you can prepare for them in advance and so save yourself from having to phone back later when you have collected other information.

32

Make sure that you find out exactly what your callers want so that you do not waste time on other matters. Do not be afraid to ask questions and don't make assumptions about what the caller is trying to say.

Ensure that you and all your staff are trained in the art of effective listening and accurate message-taking. Anyone taking a message must listen carefully to the caller and ask questions until all the information is given. Ask for difficult words to be spelt out. A note should be made of the date and time of the call as well as any action to be taken. The notes of any message should be full and accurate and passed on to the person concerned immediately.

Do not be afraid of delegating the job of answering the phone to your staff whenever possible. Not only will this increase the efficiency of your organisation but the morale of your staff will improve. Encourage and praise staff who show initiative and act effectively on incoming calls. By anticipating and preparing for calls and ensuring that other people are trained to take accurate messages you can reduce your incoming calls drastically.

33

CHECKLIST

1 Reorganise your time to avoid unwanted calls.
2 Discourage transferred calls.
3 Use a loudspeaker telephone if your hearing is poor.
4 Encourage staff to act on messages.
5 Anticipate calls.
6 Prepare for calls.
7 Take good messages and notes.
8 Train your staff.
9 Find out what callers really want.
10 Use your secretary.

3

How to get rid of unwanted callers

Tame that phone and tame your temper! It is very tempting to lose control when someone on the other end of the phone annoys you. You can't see them so letting off steam seems a safe option, but it isn't.

'Well, if I called the Wrong Number, Why Did You Answer the Phone?'

Title of a cartoon from *Men, Women and Dogs* by James Thurber.

Unwanted callers take many forms. They can be anyone from someone who has dialled a wrong number on your direct line to your Great Aunt Mary phoning for a chat. They can be someone who takes up your time with irrelevant chatter or who tries to doorstep you into making a decision when you don't want to. Anyone who uses rudeness or heavy-handedness to get their way can raise your temper to boiling point. They can be people you dislike but need to speak to. They can be salespeople making cold calls. They can be people you have met but wish to avoid speaking to. There are many reasons why a caller can be unwanted. But, however irritating or rude, you must keep calm. In this chapter I tell you how to recognise which of your calls are unwanted and explain how to deal with unwanted callers. To deal with these types of callers you need to sound assertive and in command of the situation. I tell you how to become more confident and how to stand up for yourself when taking difficult calls.

How to tread the fine line

You can rarely afford to be rude. The caller who is irritating you so much may be a good customer or a valued colleague, a potential client or a media representative. They may make you very angry but unless you know what the consequences are going to be you cannot afford to be rude, however much you might like to be.

Losing your temper at the wrong moment could lose you an order, create an abusive headline in the local paper or anger the director's mother. Don't take chances.

The only time you can afford to be rude is if you are absolutely sure of your ground and that the caller is simply making a sales cold call to you and has nothing to do with the firm and no interest in it. Unfortunately cold-calling, annoying enough on a domestic phone, is now common in the business world. It is one thing for someone who is trying to sell your firm something relevant and useful to cold call you; it is quite another for a double-glazing salesperson to call you in office time.

These types of callers invariably give a name you have never of and then launch into their spiel or else refuse to give their name or tell their business until you have promised 10 minutes of your time.

Trying to argue with these kinds of callers about who they are and what they want has no effect on them and just leaves you angry and upset. Do not waste your time with these people. You need to deal firmly with persistent callers and you may have to repeat the message often enough for them to get the meaning. Say each time they call 'I'm sorry, I can't talk now' and put the phone down. It would take a very dim person not to understand that you don't want to talk to them.

Do not listen to either of these kinds of callers. Anyone who does not tell you at once who they are, what their organisation is and what they want is suspect from the start. If they do not take a polite 'No, I'm not interested' for an answer then you are justified in being rude. You do not even need to be abusive. Simply hang up and if they call again say 'I am going to ask for security to intercept my calls'. They won't know it isn't possible and are unlikely to risk being traced.

TALKATIVE PROBLEM CALLERS

One common form of unwanted caller comes from people who have a complaint to make or an axe to grind and wish to talk to you about it at great length. These kinds of callers rarely take no for an answer and simply ignore your attempts to get rid of them. Short of putting the phone down in the middle of the call, how can you deal with them?

Rory O'Kelly, Secretary of Lewisham Community Health Council, has a lot of experience of dealing with these types of calls:

> *I get a lot of persistent problem callers. Your classic caller tends to talk at length. What they want is a statement from you. Even if you don't say anything except 'but' or 'er' they take this as encouragement to renew their speech.'*

But there is a good way of getting rid of such callers. Rory O'Kelly suggests this especially effective method:

> *Do not respond. Wait until they have said everything they want to and come to a stop. Wait in silence for three or four seconds before you reply. This makes them nervous and they will start speaking again to fill the gap. But if you repeat the silent waiting trick several times they will eventually give up. The reason this works is because callers do not have your body language or your voice to respond to.*

By letting persistent problem callers run out of steam you can get rid of them without saying something rude or losing your temper.

MALICIOUS CALLS

If you should be on the receiving end of phone calls from heavy breathers or abusive callers, put the phone down at once and tell your manager so that action can be taken. It may not be practicable to use the whistle method – that is, to keep a whistle by the phone and blow it into the receiver when the caller makes another unpleasant call. It may be effective but it is not suitable for an office situation.

Fortunately BT has a system for dealing with this type of call. Contact them as soon as the problem is obvious. They will arrange to trace the calls and will co-operate with the police in order to catch the criminal – because such calls *are* criminal. The offender can them be prosecuted. If the calls are so unpleasant and abuse that you need counselling, then BT will arrange this too. There are more details about how to deal with malicious calls later in the book.

RECEIVING COMPLAINTS

The kinds of calls we all hate to get are those which are complaining about us, the company or life in general. However unpleasant and unwelcome such calls are they must be dealt with in a calm and sensitive manner.

Customers who complain and who do not receive satisfaction from their calls pass on their dissatisfaction to their family and friends. It is better that they should make their complaint and be dealt with fairly than they should not call and your company lose a number of potential clients. Word of mouth is a powerful builder and destroyer of reputations. If you can get complaints dealt with effectively, satisfied clients will go away to praise your organisation to their friends.

So although complaints are unwanted they must be dealt with promptly and sensitively.

However, for you personally, the calls are unwanted because they cut into your work time and can annoy or upset you. If you do get angry or upset yourself this will prolong the call and you will not be able to get on with your work.

Remember these rules:

(i) Don't try to reason with someone who is very angry. Somebody who is angry and upset is not going to be amenable to reasoned argument. Your first job is to calm them down and find out what the problem is. Be a good listener. Let the caller get their problems off their chest. By listening carefully you will seem to be a friend rather than an opponent.

(ii) Don't take complaints about the company personally. It is easy to get upset by what you perceive to be a personal slight. But if you think about it the complaint is more likely to be about the company. Just because they've phoned you and are blaming you doesn't make it your fault. It simply means that they have got your name as somebody who can deal with the problem. Don't take it personally. You are not the company, even if you think you are.

(iii) If the caller is aggressive, keep calm. Your first job with an aggressive caller is to calm them down so that you can find out what is troubling them. It is impossible to have a sensible conversation with somebody who is shouting or swearing. Confine your comments to 'mm' or 'ah' until their anger is spent. Only then can you begin to talk to them constructively.

(iv) Stay as calm and objective as possible. When somebody phones to complain you may feel angry or annoyed at what they have to say. Do not let that show in your voice or words. It will not help either of you if you lose control of the situation. Try to be objective about what you are being told, even if the complaint is genuinely about you personally. Try to see the problem from the other person's point of view as well as your own so that you can give a reasoned reply.

(v) Let the caller talk until they have run out of steam. Some people make complaints when they are not angry but they do want to say a lot about it. So let them talk on until they have said everything they want to say. It will make them feel better and you can decide how to answer them.

(vi) Encourage the caller to tell you all their complaints. Often a caller will talk about many things that annoy him but the main problem may not be obvious. Encourage the caller to tell you everything about the problem that upsets or annoys them. Then it will be difficult for them to think of something else to complain about just as you have sorted the problem out.

(vii) Restate their complaints in their own words. This is a useful device. It clarifies for you exactly what the problem is and it takes the sting out of the complaint for the caller. The caller may have many different emotions involved with the problem – guilt, anger, fear, misery. By restating the problem in neutral terms it defuses the situation.

(viii) Don't offer help you can't provide or make unchecked assertions. Promising help when you can't provide it or making statements that you are unsure about will simply upset the other person more when they prove to be wrong and will not help them, you or your company. Don't be afraid to tell the caller that you will ask for a second opinion. This at least reassures them that you are doing your best to get an answer to the problem. If you do promise to help the caller, make sure that you do so. Broken promises do not inspire confidence in you or your company.

(ix) Try to find a solution. One of the best ways of getting rid of a caller who is complaining is, of course, to find a solution to the problem. You do not want to leave the caller angry and unsatisfied. They may not phone again or they may be so incensed that they call you back and other members of your staff. If you can deal with the problem yourself, do so (but see section viii). If you cannot deal with the problem yourself but know someone else who can, pass the caller on. But remember to give the other person full details of the problem so that the caller does not have to repeat themselves. This will only make them even more angry. Only pass on calls to people who really *can* help.

Helplines

Receiving complaints can be a full-time job and it is not how you should be spending your time. It may be worth your while to find out whether your company could set up one or more helplines. These are dedicated phone lines where the calls are answered by specially trained staff who can deal with most complaints, pass on more difficult complaints to the most appropriate person straight away, and deal with more general enquiries. This can save both you and your staff a great deal of time which might otherwise be spent on the phone.

Helplines engender more customer satisfaction because there is no delay in dealing with a complaint and clients do not feel that they are being passed around an office with little chance of getting a sensible response.

This is an excellent way of both improving customer relations and making your company more efficient. Many government agencies, health authorities and councils are already providing helplines as part of their efforts to comply with the Citizens' Charter.

Even if your company cannot afford to provide a large number of help-lines, it should be possible to employ one member of staff to deal with complaints and enquiries. The job would more than earn the salary paid in increased work time and good relations with your clients.

Polite alternatives

If you want to get rid of the caller but dare not risk being rude then you have a number of polite but effective options. Be careful about using these. Remember that your job when answering the phone is to provide a helpful and efficient image of yourself and your company. You must make sure that when you control your phone you do not jeopardise this by being unnecessarily rude and off-putting to colleagues and clients. Only use the more forceful and off-putting techniques if the caller has become a particular nuisance and not if they have a genuine problem.

TELL THE CALLER TO SEND A FAX

Say something polite like 'That all sounds very interesting. Why not fax it to me so that I can look over it as soon as possible.' The word 'Fax' acts like magic. It makes everything seem important and gives the information a status above its station. By asking the caller to send a fax you are in effect saying 'This information seems so important that I must have it immediately'.

Once you have a fax from the caller you will be able to see who it is from and who is sending it. Then get your secretary to screen your calls. You can instruct her to say that you are away on business if someone from the organisation named on the fax phones you. Tell her to keep saying this continually until the caller gives up. If you are on a direct line you may want to put your answer machine on to screen the calls yourself.

ASK THE CALLER TO WRITE A LETTER

A letter does not have the same immediacy and impression of importance as a fax but can be used to the same effect. By the time they have written the letter and sent it, the caller may have lost interest. Simply do not reply to the letter. If the caller phones again employ the same techniques as for the caller who sends a fax. Eventually they will go on to easier prey. After all, they cannot afford to waste time on you.

TELL THEM TO SEND MORE INFORMATION

This has become almost a shorthand for 'Please go away and leave me alone; I am not the slightest bit interested in what you have to say'. Most callers on hearing this will simply agree and hang up.

Your persistent caller will, of course, send you the information. After making a mental note of who and what firm to avoid accepting a call from, throw the information away.

TRY AGAIN LATER

This is a crafty one often used in places like Council offices. The trick, having said that, is to be away from the office for at least the rest of the day, if not longer. Ask your secretary or a colleague to tell the caller if they try again to say 'I'm sorry, Miss Roberts is still out of the office.' (Of course, you could be even more crafty and stay in the office and get them to say that anyway but your presence may make your colleagues forget.)

TRY SOMEONE ELSE IN YOUR ORGANISATION

If the caller needs to speak to someone in your firm and your temper is cracking tell them they must speak to 'Mr Jones in Department C7' and transfer them or give the name and number. This takes the onus off you to either end the call or deny the information. The caller will think he or she is being dealt with correctly and, unless they know your firm exceptionally well, cannot argue that Mr Jones will not know more about the problem than you.

If Mr Jones is a friend of yours he may be aware of what you are up to and pass the caller on to someone else. This office merry-go-round (which even genuine callers sometimes get) is almost guaranteed to put off all but the most persistent caller.

If Mr Jones does not know you he will pass the call on anyway because he knows nothing about the subject. Either way the result will be the same. Be out of the office as soon as you have transferred the call in case it gets passed back to you. You can be even more cunning and tell the caller that you will try someone else in your organisation for them. The caller will have difficulty in rejecting this offer of help. Of course, you can try someone else as promised or simply 'forget' to do so.

SERIOUSLY NOT INTERESTED

Of course, you *are* seriously not interested in receiving unwanted calls. But it is not always appropriate to tell the caller so. Do so quickly if you discover that you have an unwanted salesperson on the other end of the line. But what if it's a colleague trying to get you to agree to a

41

reorganisation of the management structure or get you to talk at a seminar which will eat into your leave?

If you cannot fob them off with an 'It sounds an interesting idea, but I'm not really the person to talk to about this' (see section iv!) then you will have to be honest and firm. In the long run it will be less hurtful to both of you. People who cannot tell by the tone of your voice that their call is unwanted are usually thick-skinned anyway.

YOU HAVE 30 SECONDS LEFT

This is one for someone with whom you are rapidly running out of patience and are likely to scream at unless they stop or go away. Try not to lose your temper – even speaking through gritted teeth will not hide your anger. It may have the advantage both of stopping you raging out of control and of conveying your annoyance, but it is not an appropriate response to any caller.

If you feel like this, say 'just a minute', hold the phone at arm's length and take a deep breath. After several breaths, and when you feel calm enough to talk normally, then resume the conversation. If you really cannot contain yourself then you must end the conversation.

When you can stand no more, simply say 'I'm going to put the phone down in 30 seconds'. Do not explain why. The caller will either think you are very busy or get the message. If they still carry on, then you lose nothing by cutting them off.

By giving a time limit of 30 seconds you are giving the caller the chance to catch on and apologise for wasting your time. If they do you can part on civil terms. If not, you have saved yourself from a continued unwanted call.

YOU CANNOT MAKE A DECISION NOW

This is a good excuse if you want to get rid of someone who wants to push you into a decision and wishes to give you a long explanation about it. Do not be bullied into making a decision that you might regret later simply in order to get rid of them. You will then have to phone them back and reverse the decision which will mean you could get embroiled in an unwanted conversation again.

You can use this excuse as a delaying tactic or as a 'Don't call us we'll call you' polite fob off. It can be used with the excuses in sections (i), (ii) and (iii) above. If you really do have to take a decision, of course, it is only common sense in any case to ask for further information before you commit yourself.

CALL BACK LATER

You cannot risk making this excuse unless you really mean to call back (so it's your mother, and you love her). Even if you have no wish whatsoever to speak to the person again, it is unfair to let them sit at the phone waiting for a call because you promised to call them. You wouldn't like it yourself.

If you do wish to speak to them again, or will have to in the course of your work, but the call is unwanted at that particular time, tell them you will call back. Give a definite time so that you do not leave them wondering whether they can risk leaving their office or not. When you call back, you will be in charge of the conversation.

43

SAY 'GOOD-BYE'

It is surprising how effective simply saying 'good-bye' in the middle of the conversation is. By doing this you leave the caller confused. Did the or she say something that implied the conversation was at an end? Have they offended you? Did they hear you properly? Did they miss a vital part of the conversation which ended it in a more normal way?

Most callers faced with this reaction in the middle of a call will retire puzzled or hurt but are unlikely to bear a lasting grudge because they will not be sure in their own minds that it wasn't something to do with them. If they are annoyed then it serves them right for driving you to use that tactic.

By using any of the above 10 techniques you will be able to avoid losing your temper at an inappropriate moment. With luck your unwanted calls will be drastically reduced.

Assertiveness on the phone

An assertive attitude on the phone will not only help you to get rid of unwanted callers but will help you control any telephone conversation and get the result you want. Learning how to sound confident and put your points across is an important part of your telephone technique. You will feel more in control and your callers will respect you.

Assertiveness is about good communication. It is the ability to make your point of view known honestly and clearly. It means saying what you mean and standing up for your rights without letting the other person override you. Assertiveness does *not* mean being rude or shouting or being aggressive. Nor does it mean that you should feel superior to other people. In fact, people who are truly assertive and have confidence in themselves get on well with their peers, their superiors and their staff. They are treated with the respect that an honest and confident outlook engenders.

An assertive attitude can be achieved without becoming unpleasant. It means being confident enough to end a conversation if it is unwanted or unproductive. At the same time it means that you can guide a conversation and come to a satisfactory conclusion without antagonising the other person. In fact you should aim to find some common ground which you can agree on. This gives you a friendly basis for the conversation and enables you to bring in any points of disagreement without sounding unpleasant 'Yes, I like the idea of a major conference in July. But I don't think that inviting the Morrison team to give a demonstration will be helpful . . .' Using the phone can reduce normally confident people to cowards. There is something about not being able to see the reaction of the person on the other end of the line that makes people unsure of themselves and apologetic. Without someone's body signals to guide them, some people become disorientated in a telephone conversation and nervous. There is the feeling that they are not quite in control. This attitude conveys itself to the recipient and they in turn will become more confident.

This diffidence is a feeling which you must learn to overcome if you are to control your phone. Without your body signals to help convey your meaning to the caller the way you use your voice and how you frame your sentences will be the only guide the caller has to your meaning and attitude. If you do not sound firm, authoritative and business-like on the phone then your calls will go on for longer than is necessary and you will make inappropriate decisions. Indecisiveness is a great time-waster in any situation, more so on a phone where you can stare up at the ceiling or scribble on the desk jotter while you are trying to gather your thoughts and the caller cannot see you.

Sounding business-like, too, helps to keep the caller under control. If you sound brisk and as if you have not got time to waste, the person you are speaking to will take his or her cue from you and speak to you in the same vein. By starting out sounding efficient you effectively nip waffling in the bud. Sounding business-like, too, also encourages you to live up to how you sound.

Many people find being assertive in their daily lives difficult enough without having to be so over the phone when you cannot gauge the other person's reactions by looking. If you feel like this it is important that you practise making your points of view clear.

45

There are a few rules to remember before you think about other tricks to make you sound assertive:

- don't prevaricate – say 'No' if you don't agree
- don't apologise for saying 'No'
- only say 'Yes' when you really mean it
- don't commit yourself to something you don't want to or can't do
- sound confident
- prepare for your calls
- don't be afraid to apologise for mistakes.

SOUND FIRM

Do not confuse sounding firm with being rude. So often somebody will say 'I believe in plain speaking' when they really mean 'I believe in being rude and calling it plain speaking'. An assertive person does not need to resort to unpleasantness to make a point. They express their feelings openly, but with enough consideration for the other person so that they do not leave a bad feeling.

Do not lose your temper or say 'shut up' if you do not agree with the other person's point of view. That is not being assertive, that is being aggressive. Instead of reaching common ground you will simply encourage the other person to lose their temper too.

Have enough confidence in yourself to sound decisive to your caller so that they feel you are in command and should fall in with your wishes. Remember they cannot see you so you can be going pink and quivering like a jelly but as long as you *sound* in control, who will know?

How do you set about sounding firm and in control on a phone? Preparation plays a big part. Make sure that you have notes of what you want to say (see the following chapters). If you know what you want to say and what you want to get out of the call if you are making it then that will give you confidence to start with.

If you are being called and you do not feel ready to cope with the call then ask them to phone back later when you have considered the problem under discussion. Do not be bullied into having a conversation when you do not feel ready to cope with it.

Use firm statements such as:

46

- 'these are the points we should discuss . . .'
- 'let's take this point first . . .'
- 'yes, let's agree to do that . . .'
- 'no, that won't work . . .'
- 'let me have the information by Tuesday, please . . .'

There is a difference between sounding assertive and sounding bossy. People can accept one while they won't the other. If you say things like 'Do that . . .' or 'We won't do that . . .' you will antagonise people. Say rather 'So you'll do that for us will you?' or 'It won't be possible for us to do that but . . .' By slightly altering the emphasis you stay in control without being aggressive.

Try using silence as an assertive 'statement'. When you have made a point do not say anything else. By keeping quiet you are saying effectively 'I have said all that I want to say and I believe I am right'.

SAYING NO

Saying 'No' is one of the most powerful assertiveness techniques. Many people are cowards when it comes to refusing to agree to another person's point of view or request. This becomes even more difficult for them when making a phone call because they cannot use body language or eye contact to indicate that they are reluctant.

The ability to say 'No' and mean it is good assertiveness. It means that the other person has to put effort into persuading you. As long as you keep saying 'No' you have the upper hand. If you feel you must soften the blow keep it short. 'No, I can't manage that.' Then stop. Remember the old adage 'Never apologise, never explain'. Obviously there are occasions when you should break that rule, but when you want to refuse something is not the time. Also remember the rule – **KISS – Keep It Short and Simple**. The longer excuse you give the more nervous and unsure you will sound and the more the other person will seek to persuade you to his or her viewpoint. So say no and mean it.

Don't be afraid of saying 'No'. It is not rude or unbusiness-like to say what you mean. Far better to say a straightforward 'No' first and then go on to say what you can do, rather than say 'I don't know about that, not at the moment anyway, I'll let you know'. That just sounds as if you are unsure of yourself and are incapable of making a decision. People will respect you far more if you are honest. No business runs efficiently if too many 'Yeses' are said to the wrong people at the wrong time about the wrong things. You may find you have committed yourself by your uncertainty to something time-consuming and unnecessary.

47

Have a sign on your phone to remind you to say 'No' more often – 'I'm sorry, it's impossible'. If it's you that is making the call you could have 'Who is paying for the time and cost of this call?' or visualise the phone bill!

Always sound as if you have the authority to make decisions. If you sound as if you are in command people will take you at 'face value' (even if they can't see you!). How are they to know that you were only promoted yesterday and haven't got the hang of things yet. *Sound* as if you know what you are doing and you will convince yourself and the person on the other end of the telephone.

HOW TO SAY 'GOOD-BYE'

Many people seem unable to end telephone conversations. They sound as if they are going to, then they start up another topic of conversation. They say 'I must be going. I'll get on with that report then, shall I? We agreed Tuesday didn't we?' and before you know it you are having the same telephone conversation all over again.

Maybe it's you who find it difficult to end the conversation. You may think that you will sound rude or abrupt. But it is far more rude to waste someone's time by carrying on a conversation that ended several minutes ago. If you made the call, then it is your duty to end it when appropriate and not to take up too much of the other person's time. When you have covered everything simply say 'That's fine. Thank you for your time. Good-bye' and put the phone down. The other person will simply be relieved that they can now get on to other things.

If you are being called and the other person does not seem inclined to go away then say 'We seem to have covered everything. I'll be in touch. Good-bye'. Put the phone down after the other person says 'good-bye'. Do not be tempted to pause for a second to see if they are going to add anything. If you do, they will and it will take longer to extract yourself.

If the other person does not respond 'good-bye', then simply repeat your good-bye firmly and put the phone down. They may want to chat but your time is more valuable than that.

Of course, if you are on friendly terms with the other person and it is your lunchtime you may enjoy a longer call, but again, make sure that when you want to end the conversation you do so firmly and quickly. To hesitate is to be lost to a new wave of talk.

Ways of saying 'good-bye':

- 'Thank you for your time – I know you're busy so I won't keep you.'
- 'Nice speaking to you, speak to you soon.'
- 'I must dash.'
- 'I'll send a fax confirming this call.'

Be polite

You don't have to be rude to end a phone conversation effectively. Be polite and if you are talking to a stranger try to use their name in your last sentence as in 'I must go now. Good-bye Miss Adams'.

Before you end a conversation on the phone briefly repeat any facts you want the other person to remember. People remember what you say at the end of a conversation more easily than any other part of it.

Remember three points:

(i) **be brief**
(ii) **be firm**
(iii) **be gone.**

Sound firm and business-like, be assertive, and say 'good-bye' promptly, and you will be in command of any phone call.

Summary

Your phone calls may be unwanted for a variety of reasons. For example, they may be time-wasting, malicious or complaints. They may also be dangerous, as in the case of callers warning of bombs.

If the phone calls are malicious or dangerous, contact the police and BT. They will advise you on the best course of action. BT can trace calls and will co-operate with the police in tracking down the caller.

If your caller is angry and complaining keep calm. Do not lose your temper. Do not try to reason with the caller or say something unpleasant. Do not take complaints about your company personally. Let the caller run out of steam and encourage them to tell you about all their concerns. Restate their complaints in their own words but don't offer to provide help unless you can do so. If you do promise to look into the matter, do so and call them back.

Get rid of callers politely but firmly by telling them to send a fax, write a letter, send more information, try again later, speak to somebody else, that you are not interested, you cannot decide now, to call back later, or by saying 'good-bye'.

Do not use excuses to get rid of a caller unless they are really unwanted or a persistent nuisance. Remember the next caller may be a nervous new client or the boss' wife!

Learn how to sound assertive on the phone. This will not only help you deal with unwanted callers but will help you keep control of any phone conversation.

Assertiveness is about good communication and sounding confident without becoming aggressive or rude. Being assertive does not mean being unpleasant. Make firm statements and learn to say 'No' and mean it. Only say 'Yes' when you really mean it. Preparing for your calls will help you feel confident. Even if the other person cannot see you they can hear the confidence in your voice.

Finally, learn how to say' good-bye' and remain polite. It is not rude to end a phone conversation when everything has been said. Remember to be brief, be firm, be gone.

CHECKLIST

1 Don't be rude unless you really have to be.

2 If your caller is angry, keep calm.

3 Don't take general complaints personally.

4 Try to use polite alternatives for getting rid of callers.

5 If you promise to call back, do so.

6 Don't make statements if you are unsure of your facts.

7 Sound confident.

8 Sound firm.

9 Learn to say 'No' more often.

10 Learn to say 'Good-bye' effectively.

4

Outgoing calls

As a busy manager you must take responsibility for your outgoing calls. Not only must you make sure that they are necessary but that using the phone is the most appropriate way of conducting your business on each occasion that you use the phone. You need to keep as much free time as possible for the more constructive work you have to do.

In this chapter you will learn how to identify which of your outgoing calls are necessary and how to reduce the number of phone calls you make. You will find out how to decide whether it is better to communicate by means other than the telephone. By learning to reschedule your calls you can free your time.

You will learn how to prepare for calls and use a call sheet. I will tell you how to deal with difficult calls and you will discover how to get hold of elusive people and salvage abortive calls.

But first of all, whenever you decide you need to make a phone call, ask yourself whether it is really necessary.

Do you really have to ring?

It is a common mistake to think that just because you have a phone sitting on your desk that you must use it. It may be the most appropriate way of conducting business for much of the time but there will be many occasions when using the phone would be more trouble than time-saving.

Think how many times you have made a phone call only to have to send follow-up information in the form of a letter or other written informa-tion. On those occasions wouldn't it have been better to have sent the letter in the first place? Then if the person you sent the letter to needed more information, he or she could phone you.

Think carefully each time before you pick up the phone. Ask yourself:

- Do I really need to make this call?
- Must I contact this person now or can it wait a day?
- Will I need to follow up a phone call with documentation?
- Will it take a long time to explain what I mean when a letter or diagram may do it better?
- Do I need to say anything at all?
- Will it take me longer to phone than to write or dictate a note?

What other methods of communicating might be quicker, clearer or more useful to you and the person you are calling? Why not consider the following ways of reducing your outgoing calls?

FAX

One of the wonders of the modern age, a fax (facsimile machine) can send documents across the world in the time it takes to make a phone call and for not much more than the cost of the call. If you have information that is best expressed on paper, such as diagrams or forms, then a fax is the best answer, especially if time is of the essence. All the phone is used for is transmitting the information and perhaps confirming the receipt. You can make any queries in a follow-up call. This eliminates at least the preliminary call.

LETTER

Why not write a letter? Socially letter-writing may be a dying art but it should be alive and well in an efficient office. Often whatever you need to be say in a phone call you can write in a letter. If the information is not urgent then a letter or hand-written note may be the best answer.

It also gives you time to think about what you want to say. So if you think that you may forget what you are saying on the phone or are a bit nervous then consider the letter option. A well thought out and typed letter on pleasant notepaper can often be more impressive than a hurried phone call. For internal use, a hand-written note is often a quick and acceptable solution.

As a manager you may well receive formal invitations to dinners or events. In those cases, unless you are specifically asked to reply by phone, it is correct to send a letter of acceptance.

Although people do not consider the post to be fast or reliable it is still the case that the Post Office delivers about 90 per cent of its letters to the recipients by the next day of posting. So don't disparage the humble letter.

Urgent letters can be sent by special delivery by the Post Office for guaranteed next day delivery. For same or overnight delivery you can use UK Datapost courier service. For fast delivery of letters to Europe use the Post Office Swiftair airmail service. This delivers letters by airmail one day earlier than the two to four days of normal airmail delivery. The advantages of a letter or fax are:

- it can be as quick
- it can be cheaper
- the documentation can be copied and filed
- a letter or fax is often more impressive than a rambling phone call
- it is easier to refer back to a piece of paper rather than try to remember a phone conversation.

53

WRITE ON YOUR ENQUIRER'S LETTER

Often a quick way of replying to someone's letter is not to reach for the phone but to write a quick note on the bottom of their letter. This has several advantages:

- it is very quick
- the recipient can see at a glance what you are replying to
- it saves paper (especially if you reuse envelopes too!).

SILENCE

This is not as silly as it sounds. Think – do you really need to make any reply at all? If the letter you have received is providing information you have asked for or asking a question which someone else can answer, you do not need to make any reply. Why phone to say 'Thank you, I got your letter and I'm looking into it'? Unless you have some really vital information to impart immediately, leave it. The other person has work to get on with too!

Planning your calls

Once you have finally decided that a phone call is necessary, do not leap immediately to the phone. The chances are you will forget what you want to say or sound muddled. Then you will sound out of control to the person on the other end of the line.

Take a little time to plan your calls. A little thought before you lift the receiver will save any amount of time and confusion later on. If you have a tendency to be nervous on the phone then it is especially important to take time to consider how you are going to approach your call.

TEN SECONDS TO SAVE 10 MINUTES

Each time you make a call take a few seconds to consider what you are going to say and how you are going to say it. Preparation beforehand will save you a lot of time later on. It really is 10 seconds to save 10 minutes!

Consider these points:

- be clear about what you want to say
- know whom you want to speak to
- have a message prepared in case the person you call is unavailable
- have any relevant paperwork to hand
- have a paper and pen
- have reminder cards with important names and facts
- take a few deep breaths beforehand and relax
- visualise the person you are talking to
- visualise a calming situation
- choose a time to phone when you are least likely to be interrupted and when the person you are calling is most likely to be in.

None of the above suggestions take very long and yet they can save a lot of unnecessary worry and time wasting. Let's look at some of them in more detail.

How to warm up for a difficult call

All of us have to make difficult calls from time to time. For example, we may have to reprimand or criticise somebody. It does us no good to put off the call because that makes us worried and makes the call more difficult to get round to. Also, if it is a problem important enough to need our attention then we should deal with it quickly so that good working practices can continue.

Deal with these difficult calls quickly and firmly so that you can get on with the rest of your day without worrying about them.

(i) Take the initiative. Don't wait for the other person to phone up about something else or you will find it embarrassing to have to change the subject and introduce a note of unpleasantness into the conversation. If you make the call then you can prepare your remarks.

(ii) Get to the point quickly. It does neither you nor the recipient a kindness to delay telling unpleasant news. Don't skirt round the subject to soften the blow – it won't. Start by saying 'My reason for calling is . . .' and tell them straight away.

(iii) Delay your reply. If a caller catches you unawares and phones you about something that you need to have thought out your remarks about, don't reply at once. Make an excuse and phone back when you have considered your answers or remarks. That way you can stop yourself saying something you wished you hadn't.

WHAT ARE YOU GOING TO SAY

Everyone has had the experience of making a phone call and being well into the conversation when the main point you wanted to make has gone out of your head. We think that we will remember what we want to say but often we don't. Even if we do remember we quite often fail to make the points of our argument in a concise and logical way. This not only means that we lose track of what we are saying but that it gives the person you are calling the advantage of being more in control of the conversation.

The way to avoid this is easy. Make sure you write down what you want to say on a piece of paper or card. Just one sentence with the main point is enough. List any other important points in numerical order underneath. Write clearly so you don't have to peer closely at the card or try to work out what you've written. Then when you are speaking on the phone you will have the main points of your conversation to hand and will not miss any out or stray from the point.

WHAT OUTCOME DO YOU WANT?

Are you going to try to reach a decision on the phone? Do you want a commitment from the other person? Do you need a definite date or an agreement to action form the person you are calling?

If you are clear from the start what result you want you can steer the conversation towards it and ask appropriate questions?

Write on your reminder card **Outcome** and then what you want. Then, at the end of the conversation, you can ask 'Shall we set a date for a meeting next week?' or 'So we agree that you will deliver the equipment on Monday 17th at 3 pm?'. When you have reached a decision then the conversation is at an end because you have got the result you wanted so you can ring off. This means that there is no time wasted with talking after you reach a decision.

HOW ARE YOU GOING TO SAY IT?

How you talk to the person you are calling is very important. Are you making a complaint and so need to be polite but firm? Have you called to apologise so you need to be straightforward and contrite? Are you calling to arrange a meeting so you need to be decisive and efficient?

Each call demands a different way of conducting the conversation. But some traits are common to all calls. You must speak clearly, say what you want to say confidently but politely and reach a decision sensibly. Your aim should be to make each phone call a good call, one that achieves what you want in the minimum of time without lacking manners. By having the points written on a card as I advised above you will already have the form of the conversation in hand and will feel less nervous.

Rules for getting what you want

You don't have to rant and rave to get your message across. But there are some rules to remember if you want to ensure that you get what you need from each call, however difficult to make.

(i) **Know exactly what you want.** If you don't know you won't be able to explain succinctly to the person you are calling.

(ii) **Check your facts.** Be sure that what you say is correct and that you have any evidence you need to hand.

(iii) **Telephone rather than write.** This can be a good move if making a complaint, because it gets a more immediate response. This is one time you should use the phone.

(iv) **Use fax or telex.** If the main points of your argument are complicated, fax or telex them to the other person so that you both have them in front of you when you call.

(v) **Be persistent.** Don't accept an excuse for not being given what you want. Keep repeating your demand politely but firmly.

(vi) **Keep calm.** Don't get personal or lose your temper.

(vii) **Go to the top.** Talk to the most senior person possible. If you are having difficulty getting something done or need to complain make sure that you talk to somebody in a position to do something about it. Ask their receptionist for the name and title of the person in charge.

57

If you need to leave a message, either with a secretary or on an answer machine, make sure you speak clearly and spell out difficult names. Remember the acronym **KISS – Keep It Short and Simple**. Cut out any jargon and use plain English so that your message is quite clear. If it is an answer machine you can dispense with the niceties of 'hello' and 'good morning' but you must leave a date and time so that the listener can tell when you phoned. Don't forget to leave your own name too. If speaking to someone's secretary, don't waste their time with idle chat but do remember the courtesy of saying 'thank you'.

USING A CALL SHEET

Keeping a call sheet is an invaluable way of keeping track of your calls. On it you can write the date and time of your call, whom you tried to speak to, the points you wanted to make and anything important that transpired from the phone conversation. This piece of paper can easily be filed and referred to again on any subsequent occasion when you need to phone the same person.

Make sure that your call sheet is a standard size for easy filing. A4 is a good size. It is large enough to contain all the necessary information and at the same time it is the standard size for all European paperwork. Smaller A sizes (e.g. A5) would work but would be too small to be easily readable and would get lost in any standard filing system unless there were special files available. But make life easy for yourself, A4 is best.

The sheet should include:

- company name
- department
- your name

With spaces for:

- name of person you are calling
- date of call
- time of call
- main points to be made in call
- references to any related paperwork
- references to any previous relevant phone calls
- notes made during call
- action to be taken.

A suitable call sheet is illustrated in Fig. 4.1.

NOTE-TAKING WHILE SPEAKING

It is vital that you take notes of anything important said while you are on the phone. You may think that you will remember what the caller says, but you won't. Any busy manager has 101 things to think about during any one day and what is said during a phone conversation is just another set of facts to file away at the back of your busy mind. If you take notes while talking on the phone this will not only fix the conversation in your mind but will act as an aide-mémoire when you next refer to it. You can file the notes in order of priority, pass them to someone to act upon or put them in your in tray for further action.

When taking notes while on the phone make sure that you ask for the spelling of any name you're unsure of and write it down in capitals (very important if your normal writing is largely unreadable except to yourself!). Repeat important points to give yourself time to make a note of them. Write down anything you agreed upon or agreed to do with any deadline dates. Then make sure that you take the appropriate action to follow up your notes.

EAGLE ENTERPRISES

P.O. BOX 432 – NORTH DOWN, WESTSHIRE WS1 9SC

TO:	
FROM:	DEPARTMENT:
DATE:	TIME:
SUBJECT:	

MAIN POINTS:

RELATED PAPERWORK:

CALL NOTES:

ACTION:

Fig. 4.1 Sample call sheet

HOW TO SALVAGE ABORTIVE CALLS

Sometimes you will make calls and get no positive response. It could be that:

- the person you are calling is out
- you got angry and didn't finish the call
- you upset the person you were calling
- you got cut off
- you didn't reach any decision
- you forget to record a vital piece of information
- you forgot to phone back when promised.

If any of these things has happened do not despair. You can salvage abortive calls by taking immediate and effective action.

If the person you were calling was out, ask whoever answers when they will be back and make a note to phone back then. If there is no answer and the matter is urgent phone back every 15 minutes until you get a reply. Get your secretary to do this.

If you got angry and didn't finish the call take a deep breath, calm down and decide what you wanted to say. Then phone back and apologise. It is better to apologise even if you think the other person is in the wrong because that gives the other person the feeling that they can be more receptive to what you have to say. Then calmly say your piece and try to come to a conclusion without losing your temper again. If you think you are going to get angry again, say so and ask if you can phone back later when you are feeling calmer.

The same thing applies if you upset the person on the other end. You may not have meant to but if you did, you must be the one to make amends. Some people find the phone a nerve-wracking machine in any case and so any misunderstanding seems magnified. Don't stand on your dignity, phone back and make amends.

If you get cut off, phone back straight away. If you get an engaged tone, the other person may be trying to call you again so put the receiver down and wait a few minutes before trying again. If there seems to be a fault on the line, ask the operator to check the line. If you still can't get through again then you may need to fax or write to the person concerned.

If you talked on the phone but reached no decision sit down and work out what decision you needed. Was it a date for delivery? An agreement to a course of action? A decision about a report? Then phone back and ask for a decision. Do not get side-tracked and hang on until the person you are calling has come to a decision. If they need to talk to someone else first arrange to call back at a specific time. This stops them failing to call you.

You may have forgotten to record a vital piece of information when you were talking. Phone back at once and ask for it. Don't be afraid of being thought a fool. You will look even more foolish if you go into that important meeting without the information when it is so easily obtainable.

Remember the old adage 'Never apologise, never explain'. A quick, 'Hello again, Jack. Could you just tell me the date we are going to meet Fred?' will be quite sufficient and waste nobody's time. Think how much more time you will waste in explanations and delay if the chairman hears that you failed to get the information.

If you forgot to phone someone back when promised do it as soon as you remember. Do not say 'I forgot to phone then so it's too late now'. If it was important enough for you to agree to phone back then it is important enough to do so as soon as possible.

61

Make a morning a phone morning

Do not let phone calls pile up until you feel overwhelmed by them. Why not give over a morning to making all the calls that you need to make for the next few days. That will ensure that you make them all in good time, that you do not forget anyone and that you make follow-up calls straight away.

First of all, make a complete list of all the calls you need to make. Note what decisions need to be made with each call and what action you expect to make afterwards.

Work with another person, perhaps your secretary or another manager engaged in a complementary area. One of you can make the outgoing calls and the other person can be briefed to handle the incoming calls. Obviously, for this to work you need phones on two separate lines available. In this way there should be no excuse for missing any calls.

Each person should have a call sheet for each phone call to be made so that no important points are missed. Make sure that there is a plentiful supply of paper and pens so that there is no excuse for not noting any important points.

Afterwards see if any incoming and outgoing calls are related and make final calls back to tie any loose ends together. Try to get someone to shield your room so that you are undisturbed by personal callers. Pick a time of day when most of the people you are phoning will be in. In some firms, for instance, most people are in work by 8 am and so between 8 and 9 am is a good time to call. You can call others later in the morning. List your calls in order so that you don't waste time. If the person you are calling is out, leave a message or arrange to phone back later in the morning if possible.

When you ask people to phone you back, remember to give the number of the phone your colleague is using to receive the call-backs and incoming calls that morning.

Where you need to take action and you can do so with another phone call, make that call straight away. Any action that you must complete on another day should be clearly noted and put in a special place on your desk so that you can follow it up as soon as possible.

Make sure that whoever is working in tandem with you during the morning's phone-in is fully briefed to handle the call-backs and can take or make decisions on your behalf. Make sure they are fully aware of any situations in which they *must* refer the caller back to you. Get them to make a full note of the problem and to refer it to you as soon as you are free so that you can phone back quickly to sort it out.

Also make a note of any calls that need a reply or information sent by fax or letter. Dictate replies to these as soon as you can and then ideally send them off the same day. This frees the rest of your working week and speeds up any transactions. One morning spent efficiently on the phone can free up a large part of your working week.

Why not a phone afternoon?

Although I have talked about a phone *morning* you may want to make it a phone afternoon because phone calls are cheaper after midday. But consider when the people you are phoning are most likely to be there. If they are usually in the mornings, then it is a waste of time and money trying to phone them in the afternoon because you will have to phone back the next day. It may be more cost-effective in the long run to phone them during the morning. Even though each individual call will be more expensive there will be less abortive ones and less time wasted.

Obviously, if you can be sure of getting people in the afternoon then this will save your company money and you should encourage your staff to phone after lunch.

How to get hold of elusive people

Sometimes, in spite of all your efforts, it seems impossible to get hold of the people you need to speak to on the phone. They may:

- be out
- be in but guarded by their secretary
- be in later
- be in and out and no-one is sure exactly when they will be around
- be on holiday or ill
- have left a deputy in charge.

In all these instances it is perseverance that pays. For example, if the person you are calling is out and there is no-one in his or her office to answer the phone, you will simply have to keep trying. You can also try phoning another department in the same organisation to find out where and when that person will be back or if there is someone else you can speak to.

Do not be put off by someone's secretary. It may be that she has been instructed to deal with your query. If so, and you do not need to speak directly to her boss, talk to her and ask her to tell her boss.

If you do need to speak to her boss, give a message and ask her to get her boss to phone back urgently. Another good trick is to phone at lunchtime when secretaries are out. A good manager often works through his or her lunch hour and eats sitting at their desk. They then have their phones transferred to their office and answer calls themselves.

If the secretary is being obstinate, keep calling back at 15 minute intervals – she may well get fed up and put you through. But think carefully about whether it is worth antagonising her.

If you are told that the person you are calling will be in later, make a note of it and phone back five minutes after they are supposed to be in. Do not leave it later than that or they may go out again.

If the person you are trying to get hold of is in and out of the office all day and you seem to keep missing them you will have to try the 15 minute calling technique. Otherwise ask their secretary to call you as soon as they have appeared back in the office. Alternatively fax them and ask them to call you urgently.

If the person is ill or on holiday there is nothing you can do until they return. Make sure you find out when that is and make a note in your diary to phone them. If you need a decision on something quickly then you must ask to speak to whoever is in charge while that person is away.

If the substitute is simply minding the office and is not empowered to make the necessary decisions then go over their head and ask to speak to their boss. Explain the situation, ask for a decision and say that you will phone to confirm it with the person who deals with it as soon as they are back.

Only ask for the phone number of the person's home or holiday destination if the problem is very grave and cannot be dealt with any other way. You will not be thanked for badgering someone sick or on holiday unless the matter is urgent. By doing so you could ruin your good relations with the organisation.

If you are phoned at home resist the temptation to be rude, however irritating it may be. Make sure that in future you instruct your secretary not to hand out your phone number to anyone except people you have authorised and under strict circumstances.

If a deputy has been left in charge then you may be able to deal directly with them. If they do not have the power to deal with you then you must phone their superior back as soon as they are available. Do not rely on people phoning you back if the matter is important because they might miss your deadline.

TRY OUT OF OFFICE HOURS

If you think that the person is around but you simply cannot get hold of them during a normal day, trying phoning just out of office hours (i.e. outside 9 to 5 on weekdays). Many people get into the office early or stay late to catch up with work quietly or to be able to take time off in lieu if they work flexi-hours. This is often a good time to get hold of people and you can both talk in comparative quiet.

LEAVE FULL MESSAGES

Try leaving very full messages for elusive people and follow these up with messages sent by fax so that they cannot say they did not receive your call. This may encourage them to take a few minutes to sit down and call you back.

TRY WRITING

If you still fail to catch up with someone on the phone then write a letter giving full details of what you want to say. Follow this up with a request for them to phone you as soon as they can. This may encourage them to get in touch with you or at least dictate a reply.

As a last resort try some cold-calling techniques to get through to people who try to keep you at arm's length.

COLD-CALLING TECHNIQUES

When you need to get through to someone and it is proving difficult to do so, take a tip from salespeople and try the following tricks:

- dial the number yourself – don't ask someone else to do it for you
- ask the company receptionist for the title of the person you want to speak to if you are not sure
- when you want to get through to the person's secretary, ask for your contact by name, i.e. 'Ms Jones, please' or by title, 'the Director Ms Jones, please' and you are more likely to be put through
- if your contact's secretary answers, ask for your contact by name again but use the first name as well, i.e. 'Samantha Jones, please'
- use your full name and the full name of the person you want to speak to: it sounds more familiar and as if you know them well.
- when you have asked to be put through to somebody say 'Thank you' as this implies that you don't expect to be asked any more questions
- if asked 'From where' say the name of the place, not your company
- if asked to give your company's name, do so but add that it is in connection with e.g. a letter or some particular business

- try saying 'It's too complicated to tell you in detail. I need to speak to Sally Jones about it'
- say 'I'm returning Fred Parson's call': this will get you through to most people at once unless their secretary is particularly alert, in which case she will say 'It's Marie Canty returning your call'; if her boss says 'Who?' then you've lost
- if the above tactic fails try saying 'I got a message to speak to Bill Hagg. Didn't it come from this office? Perhaps I could have a word with Bill and sort it out?'
- if your contact is unavailable say you will call back and ask the most convenient time to do so: don't leave it up to your contact – *you* must be in control
- give your name when you reach the person you are calling and state your reason for calling straight away
- keep repeating who you want to speak to and what about
- do not take the first 'No' for an answer
- do not give up until you have received three negative replies
- say 'Miss Smith is expecting my call'
- say 'Such and such an organisation asked me to call Mr Jones'
- say 'I'm phoning about the such and such business' as if the person you are calling should know about it
- say 'Is Mr Richards in now?' as if he has been waiting for you to call
- say 'This is important' at least three times.

Try all or some of these techniques if the person you are calling seems reluctant to talk to you or his or her secretary declines to put you through. Once through state your business quickly and confidently. Try not to give the other person time to ask what you are calling for. Once you have stated your business then the onus is on the other person to comment or make a decision.

Summary

Not all your outgoing calls are necessary. If you do not need to say anything important or the call can wait for a day, do not make it. Be ruthless about jettisoning those calls which are time-wasting or which can be dealt with by other means.

Whenever possible, use some means other than the phone for getting your message across. You could write a letter, send a fax, jot a note on your enquirer's letter or simply do nothing at all.

Planning your calls will save you time both by reducing your time on the phone and by creating space in your working day. Prepare for your calls carefully. Ten seconds can save you 10 minutes: know what you want to say and what you want to achieve; have writing equipment, diary and relevant paperwork to hand; have a reminder card with a few important facts and names on it; and practise a few calming techniques.

Prepare for difficult calls by taking the initiative and phoning first. Get to the point quickly and don't put off making difficult calls – they will only seem worse.

To make the most of your calls be well-prepared, keep calm and be persistent.

Design and use a call sheet with room for details of the caller (you), who the call is for and notes about relevant paperwork and action to be taken. Take careful notes during the conversation.

67

Abortive calls can be salvaged. If you get cut off, redial. If you got angry, apologise. If you have forgotten an important point, have forgotten to make a return call, or need a decision, phone back immediately.

Try to make most of your calls during one period of time, such as a morning, so that you can keep the rest of the day free for other work. Get someone to help you by taking your incoming calls on another line. Try to plan your calls for a particular part of the week.

Don't be put off by elusive people. If you need to talk to them urgently, try calling them at unusual times. If they are in their office but reluctant to speak to you, try cold-calling techniques to get through to them and keep their attention. Use full names when calling so that their secretary thinks you know them. Say that you have a message to phone them or that they are expecting your call. If you still can't get through, leave very full messages. Be persistent. Your outgoing calls can be drastically reduced by ruthless pruning and proper preparation, but make any important or difficult calls promptly.

CHECKLIST

1 Make sure your phone call is really necessary
2 Use alternatives to the phone if possible

3 Prepare for each call

4 Know what you are going to say

5 Know what outcome you want

6 Keep a call sheet for each phone call

7 Take notes while speaking on the phone

8 Don't give up on abortive calls

9 Plan a morning of phone calls to save time

10 Try cold-calling techniques with elusive people

Technology to take the strain

Modern managers are fortunate in that they have a number of technical devices and phone operating systems that can help them to take the strain of incoming phone calls. Many of these devices have the advantage that important information is conveyed quickly or stored without loss. These devices vary from complex call ordering systems to simple answering aids. The busy manager can use one or several of these machines or systems together to help control incoming calls. Some of these technological innovations will help deal with your outgoing calls too. A few will help you keep in touch with your office while you are away from it.

Although these machines and systems are enticing and can do a genuinely useful job, beware of using them as time-wasting toys. For example, you may find it convenient to get other people to play with their fax to save you making or receiving unnecessary phone calls, but only use *yours* when you have to.

This chapter will tell you about the most useful modern technology available for keeping your phone calls under control and freeing your time for more valuable work, and will take a look at the most useful of the modern telephone answering systems and machines. It will explain how they work, and how they can be useful to the busy executive who needs to keep his phone calls under control. It will not only discuss the machines and systems which can be used in the office but also those which enable you to keep in touch from elsewhere in your building or even away from it.

Before we look at these machines and systems in detail let us consider how many machines you actually need on your desk. Obviously, you have a telephone handset. But should you have more than one? And how many machines do actually need?

69

How many handsets?

Cartoons and films often use the cliché of high-flying executives having many phone handsets on their desks. Several phones invariably ring at once and this shows how important they are to have so many people trying to contact them.

You may yourself think that having more than one handset on your desk will increase your efficiency because more people can contact you. In fact, only one person at a time can phone you down one line. With the help of such systems as conference calling you can arrange for several people to be able to speak on the same line. But special arrangements need to be made for this. Normally one person speaks to one other person down a phone line. So far from making it easier for you to speak to more people, you can only speak to the same number of people as usual, that is *one.*

It is, of course, possible to have more than one direct line to your desk. But would this really be an advantage? Think about what would happen if one phone rang while you were speaking on the other one. You could, of course, ask your secretary or the operator to keep them on hold – but you can do that anyway with one incoming line and a call-waiting system which is discussed later in this chapter.

You could speak to both people alternately, but this is only useful if you need to discuss something with them both. Most of your 'double' calls will be about separate subjects. With one line you can arrange for call-conferencing if you need to have a discussion with several people at once.

Without a sophisticated holding system on the other phone you would have to lift it off the hook and leave it with the microphone face up if you did not want to lose the caller. So that caller would hear everything you were saying on the other phone.

All in all it should be obvious that you can manage perfectly well with only one phone for most of the time. If you need to speak to more than one person at once on the phone you can make arrangements to do so. You can, and should, be making arrangements for other people to take and receive many of your calls so they can use their own phones. One telephone handset on your desk is ample.

By now you will have realised that far from indicating someone at the top, many handsets on a desk shows an inefficient way of working and a cluttered mind. The only excuse for having more than one handset is if you need a separate line for emergency calls or for your family. Somebody like an MP or doctor may find a second line necessary.

Most people only need one handset. At your desk there is only you. (Unless you share a desk, in which case it is more sensible to have a phone each if possible.) One phone is more than enough. After all, how many people can you speak to at once? You only need one phone and a sensible way of controlling it, which is what this book is about.

HOW MANY MACHINES?

You also cannot work efficiently at your desk if you clutter it with many bits of machinery, however useful you think they are.

You may think you need the following:

- telephone
- answering machine
- computer
- fax
- photocopier

71

Certainly, why not? But eliminate anything you can combine or do without or you will not have room to put any paper, which the modern office still needs.

Do you really need your own photocopier? If you have a fax then this will do low-level personal copying. For anything else you can use a main office machine.

Only get a computer if everyone else in your organisation is working on one and it will be cost-efficient and time-saving.

You can now combine a phone, answering machine and fax. This together, possibly with a computer, is all you need.

Systems to save you time

Although you may only have one telephone handset on your desk there are many machines and systems which can save you time and keep callers at bay if necessary. Some machines will make repeat calls for you if you need to contact someone urgently. Consider using one or more of the following technological aids to increase your phone efficiency.

CALL WAITING

This system means that if a caller phones you and you are engaged they will hear a message asking them to hold on. You will hear a bleep to let you know that someone else is on the line. You can put the original caller on hold to talk to this new person or switch between the two.

This can save you time if the new caller has relevant information for the first person because you can deal with both people at once.

Using this system also means that you can personally reassure a client or colleague who may be exasperated if left on hold by the switchboard operator or have got through to an engaged signal on your line.

Some callers in that situation may simply ring off and not bother to phone again. If your business relies on personal contact you cannot afford to lose callers, so a call-waiting system may be the answer for you.

However, it can increase your incoming calls because the new caller, instead of ringing off and trying again another time, will hold on and you will have to speak to them straight away.

You can, of course, cut them off and decide not to talk to them then. But in many ways it is a useful tool because it means that you can get a lot of incoming calls dealt with at once.

CALL DIVERSION

You can arrange to have calls to your office number automatically diverted to another extension. This is useful if you expect to be in another part of the building for a greater part of the day. It also enables you to ensure that important calls are not lost by enabling your secretary of a colleague to receive your calls if you are away.

Call diversion is also an excellent way of ensuring some peace and quiet if you have to get on with some important work undisturbed.

CALL FORWARDING

If you are out of your office building and need to ensure that important incoming calls reach you then you can divert them to another phone by pressing a few buttons. This is particularly useful if you are out and about and are using your mobile phone. You could also divert your calls to your home number, for example, if you were working from home on a particular day.

As with call waiting, you need to be able to anticipate whether you are likely to be receiving important calls. Planning your day and anticipating your incoming calls is part of managing your phone (as I have discussed in the previous chapter). Using these systems can help you do so more effectively.

CALL SEQUENCING

This is a system that holds calls in order of calling and allows a company to keep a caller on the line until the calls in front have been dealt with. It is often accompanied by music, usually of a repetitive and boring kind. Even when the music is acceptable, hearing the same short piece several times can put people off.

If you are allowed a say in whatever music is provided, try to find something of reasonable length and lively character. You don't want to bore or irritate your callers into hanging up. Nor do you want to send them to sleep!

Although this is a useful aid to call management you should not keep the callers waiting in a long call queue without some indication of how long they will have to wait or an invitation to call back later. Where they have accepted a wait the telephonist should break in and say 'Thank you for holding' every few minutes so that the client hears a human voice and does not feel neglected.

It is important to remember that even in this day and age people still make calls from public phone boxes. It may not be only clients who need to do this. Some busy executives may have forgotten their mobile phones or they may waiting for their company to issue them with one. It is important that such calls are answered as quickly as possible.

You should *not* leave call sequencing on out of office hours. It has been known for callers to phone towards the end of the day and to hold on to the phone listening to the music for ages before it dawns on them that everyone has left. This does not make for good customer relations.

At night an answering machine should leave a message saying 'This is Galon Company. There is nobody here to answer your call but if you leave your name, number and message after the tone someone will call you tomorrow'. The machine should be checked first thing in the morning and someone *must* call back.

If your answering machine is on a direct line then your usual massage will suffice.

ANSWERING MACHINES

These machines are commonplace now in most organisations and are useful both for individual executives and as a central 'voice' for the organisation. Answering machines contain a tape that, when the phone rings, plays a message from the owner and then records a message from the caller which the owner can play back later. An answering machine can either be a separate machine or combined with a telephone or fax machine.

These machines are very useful for a number of reasons.

- you can leave the phone and listen to messages later
- you can stay in the office and let the phone take the calls without having to disrupt your work
- on some machines you can hear who is calling and decide whether to answer the phone or not
- you can record information for callers which means you do not have to ring them back.

If you have an answering machine and nobody, such as a secretary, to answer the phone for you, then get into the habit of switching on your machine every time you leave the room. This may seem time-consuming but should soon become an automatic reaction. You can then be sure that you will not have missed any important message (including that one from your spouse).

You can play back the machine when you have time. Bear in mind that the tapes in the machines are small and can only hold a certain number of messages. Because nobody can tell when you actually heard the messages you are free to phone back when it is convenient to you.

You can save a lot of work time by switching on the machine while you are still in the office. If you have an important piece of work to finish and cannot afford to be disturbed by answering phone calls at that point, put the answering machine on and then ignore the bell whenever it rings. You can reply to the messages when your work is finished.

Some machines have a call monitoring system where you can hear the caller even though they cannot hear you. This is useful if you think that you may want to answer some calls but not others. Nobody can tell whether you are in the office or not until you pick up the phone and turn the machine off.

If there is any concern in an office about the safety of staff, they can use an answering machine to weed out crank or anonymous callers.

The message facility on an answering machine has other uses besides leaving the usual message of 'This is Ms Andrews' desk. Please leave

soon as possible.' If you need to let clients know where you will be you can alter the message to say 'Mr Fall will be out of the office this morning. Clients who wish to talk about the Egg account can reach him on the following number . . .' or 'Miss Lacy is away this week. Please talk to Harry Conn on extension 456 or phone back after January 10th'.

You can, if necessary, personalise the message. 'If that is Mr Smith please send in your tender by March 16th. Otherwise please leave your name, number and message after the tone.' When deciding what message to leave on your machine for callers, remember to ask the caller to tell you the date and time of the call. Just as the caller cannot tell when you will listen to the message, you cannot tell when their message was left unless they say so. It is not something that people normally do, so you may want to remind them.

It may, for example, be important to know that Marge phoned at 3 pm on Tuesday with a message to call back the same day. If you don't know when she called you may phone back too late to be useful. If this happens with a client you could lose their custom.

If your answering machine is centrally placed in the office then arrange for a member of your staff or your secretary to transcribe the messages on to individual call sheets at regular intervals, perhaps first thing in the morning and immediately after lunch. The messages can then be delivered to the individuals concerned. Your secretary can do the same for your personal machine. If you want the convenience of a answering machine but do not want to hear the calls or transcribe the messages yourself you can save yourself time by putting the machine on your secretary's desk.

A combined phone and answering machine is the more efficient machine to have in an office, otherwise your desk will become cluttered with too many bits of machinery.

Some machines enable you to listen to your messages when you are out by dialling and speaking into a phone using a Remote Voice Sequence. A more advanced version of this technique is an interrogator. This is a device which you can buy separately and use in a similar way. By dialling a special code you can hear your messages, and also reprogram and reset your machine from a distance.

THE FAX

This is the wonder of the modern office age and is rapidly becoming a vital piece of office equipment. The ability to send writing, diagrams, pictures and photographs over vast distances via the phone line has speeded up communications, even if it hasn't reduced paperwork. The fax can be a separate machine, combined with a phone, or even combined with a phone and answering machine.

Fax machines usually print their messages on thermal paper which may fade or curl but plain paper faxes are now more readily available, although still more expensive.

How will a fax help you to control phone calls? One way is by asking people to fax you information instead of phoning. The fax is the new office toy and people love using it. Your answering machine message could say 'If what you need to tell me can be sent by fax the number is . . .'. Just making your fax number generally available to clients will reduce phone calls while they play with the machine!

If you have a fax card in your computer at work you can store messages in the computer until you are ready to look at them.

If you have a fax machine make sure you or your secretary check it first thing in the morning and whenever you return to the office in case you have been sent something while you were away. You can then deal with the documentation at your leisure.

PAGERS

Pagers are small boxes that you carry with you. When you are needed, someone can phone your special pager number and you will hear a bleep on your unit. You can then phone your office to receive the message. If your pager has a screen, you then look at the number or message on your screen and can respond accordingly. Some multiple tone pagers enable you to tell where the message originated by the difference in tone.

Pagers should be used with discretion in social situations. Only doctors or other professionals who are needed in an emergency should allow the bleeping of their pager to interrupt occasions such as concerts or dinners.

VOICEBANKS

These are another way that you can keep in touch with your office when you are out and about. They can also save you from having to make repeated calls to any one number. A special bureau operates voicebanks. Your voicebank unit is about the same size as a pager and lets you know that there is a message for you. Anyone calling your voicebank number will get a recorded message from a special computerised unit attached to your phone system asking them to leave their own message for you. When they have left a message you will hear a bleep on your unit. When you hear the bleep you can hear your messages by dialling the voicebank number plus your PIN.

By using a voicebank you can be informed when a message you leave is cleared by the recipient. Urgent messages can be placed in order at the front of the queue. If you have a very important message for somebody the system can be asked to call their number at repeated intervals thus saving you or your secretary time.

Like pagers, voicebanks should not be used in social situations.

ELECTRONIC MAIL

Most managers now have a computer on their desk. If it has a modem connected to the phone it can send and receive messages either to a communal computer terminal or a personal computer elsewhere. This acts as an electronic notice board where you can 'pin' messages. By letting people know what your number is you can be sure that people who can use this system will be tempted to do so rather than phone you.

Again you can store the messages until you are ready to deal with them.

The disadvantages are:

- the system is expensive – a signing on fee and then payment per minute
- your computer needs be on all the time which wastes money and can be distracting
- if the message screen is not uppermost on the computer screen you may forget to look for messages.

If you do have computers at work this system is worth looking into.

Tessa Jowell MP, makes full use of available technology:

First home. We have two telephone lines, one for the family on which there is no answerphone and a second which is my 'work and messages' line which is widely available. The message on the answerphone does, however, direct people if they phone during the day to the House of Commons as this means that they will reach me more quickly. One other point about managing the phone at home; we did recently have a 'call waiting' put on the line – essential with four children.

At the House of Commons I have three lines: one a dedicated fax line, one a number which is given out to anyone who wants to get hold of me, and then another line which is exclusively for my use or the children should they need to contact me in an emergency. This number is not given out in order to ensure that it is not constantly engaged. My public number is very heavily used and we probably receive about 40–60 telephone calls on it a day. If people cannot get through because it is engaged they can have the alternative of leaving a message with the highly efficient House of Commons answering service who will then find me with a white slip or give me a pink copy slip 'off the board' – a message board for members in the members' lobby.

MOBILE PHONES

Strictly speaking, mobile phones are phones which are fixed into cars. But most people refer to all portable, cordless phones as 'mobile'.

There are three types of these 'mobile phones' – *mobile phones* which are permanently fixed into a car, *portable phones* which can be carried anywhere and use a battery, and *transportable phones* which can be used in or out of a car.

Do not confuse mobile phones with *cordless phones*. These need a base unit connected to a telephone line and can only work within a few hundred metres of the base unit. They have their uses for people who need to move around the office and still use a phone.

None of us have escaped hearing about these phones. The portable kind are small battery-powered phone handsets which contain press buttons for dialling and usually a message screen. They are small enough to fit in a briefcase or coat pocket. As they are cordless they can be used anywhere within range of a large number of small areas (telephone 'cells'). Ubiquitous and useful, they are now an everyday part of the communications scene in may organisations.

Tessa Jowell MP, became a convert to mobile phones when selected as a Parliamentary candidate:

> *When I was a candidate I had a phone put in my car. Like most people I had always hated them but now I find it invaluable to keep in touch with the office, let the family know when I am on my way home, and to warn people I may be meeting if I am stuck in traffic. That number is also freely available since I like using driving time to catch up with phone calls and arrangements.*

Mobile phones have many and varied uses. They:

- enable you to call the office from anywhere
- enable you to be contacted when you are out of the office
- act as reminder calls
- enable you to contact your office answering machine
- mean you can take a phone anywhere
- you can use a phone in a car.

The advantages are:

(i)   you do not lose orders by being out.

(ii)   you can be contacted immediately in an emergency.

(iii)   you can keep up to date with messages

(iv)   you can instruct your staff from anywhere – (it keeps them on their toes!)

In spite of what the press says, it is most unlikely that your mobile phone will be bugged. Thousands of calls are made all the time every day – the chances of yours being singled out and being recorded are remote.

But a mobile phone does have certain disadvantages:

- the phones use batteries which have to be replaced or re-charged. If you forget, your phone goes dead
- some mobile phones have limited ranges
- they are very expensive
- you cannot say you didn't receive the call
- you get interrupted at inconvenient moments (such as the theatre) unless you switch it off.

Most mobile phones have number storage facilities to save you taking your telephone book with you and some have message screens for receiving messages either in the form of a number to ring or a few words. Both these attributes make them useful when you are moving around a lot and need to keep in touch with the office. Some of them can be adapted for use as car phones with the addition of a special car kit.

You must take care when using them. It is obviously not polite to use them during social occasions such as the opera or a dinner. Only a doctor should need to have one during those times for emergencies. If you will be in a situation where someone may need to contact you urgently, then it is more appropriate to give the number of where you will be so that you can be contacted with the minimum of inconvenience and fuss to other people. In the same way, you should not make calls in social situations.

If you want to keep mobile phones under control, then use them sensibly. Use them to contact the office if you really need to, but keep the outgoing calls to a minimum. Instruct your secretary only to contact you with certain calls:

(i) emergencies

(ii) *urgent* business

(iii) domestic calls specified by you.

Keep any other business until you are back at the office.

If you arrange to call in to the office at specified times then this will reduce the need for your office to contact you.

In cars, mobile phones can be dangerous. In spite of what you may see in the films, you are not allowed to make calls from a hand held microphone or telephone handset while your car is moving. You can understand how dangerous it is to make calls from a car while going at 70 mph down a motorway. If you want to phone from your car you must pull over and stop.

If you have a fixed, neck slung or clipped-on microphone then you must make sure that it does not distract you from the road. And *never* stop on the hard shoulder of a motorway to take or make a call, however urgent.

If you are trying to phone someone on a mobile phone number then you must be considerate. If you discover that the recipient of your call is driving along a motorway, do not continue with the call. Say you'll call back and then do so when you think they will be safely out of the car. You do not want to be the cause of distracting them from their driving and causing an accident or death.

Trying to phone when stopped at traffic lights is another no go. You may hold up traffic or try to keep phoning while starting up. Don't do it. Not only will you get into trouble with the police but you may cause an accident. There is no point in getting extra phone calls if you end up under a lorry and unable to collect the extra business.

81

Although bugging your phone is unlikely, you may be picked up accidentally on local radios. Also if you are in a public place instead of using a phone in the privacy of a phone box you may get overheard by the public. It is sensible not to discuss confidential or sensitive matters in public on a mobile phone. Take the details and then ask the caller if you can phone them back at a more convenient time.

Because mobile phones are a status symbol they are likely to get stolen. They may fit in your pocket but they are easy to steal or take if you leave the phone in your jacket when you take your jacket off. If you need to use a mobile phone then you will have to keep it in an inside or breast pocket or briefcase and keep an eye on it. It is an expensive instrument to lose.

It should go without saying that leaving a portable phone on view in your car is foolish. If you cannot take it with you then leave it out of sight in the boot of the car. If it is stolen report its loss to your company and the police immediately. Make sure that you or your security department has marked it with invisible ultraviolet markers before you use it, so that if someone recovers it, it can be traced back to your company.

Summary

You need to use modern technology to keep your calls under control, whether they are incoming or outgoing. But beware of finding the machines themselves so exciting that you waste time playing with them.

Do not have more machines on your desk than you need – combine them if possible. Only have one telephone handset unless you need an emergency line.

There are many useful systems for controlling incoming calls. Consider using call waiting which enables you to keep a caller on hold during another call and talk to both callers if necessary; call diversion to steer incoming calls to another extension; call forwarding to direct calls to an outside phone; and call sequencing to hold calls in order until you are ready to answer them.

Useful machines for your office include an answering machine to record messages from incoming callers; a fax to send and receive documents and a computer set up to send and receive electronic mail (e-mail).

If you need to keep in contact with your office when you are away from it you can carry a pager which will let you know you should contact your office; a voicebank unit to enable you to send and receive messages; an interrogator for your answering machine so that you can hear your messages and reset it from a distance; or a portable or mobile phone.

Use machines efficiently and encourage your callers to use them too.

If you are using voicebanks, pagers or mobile phones, make sure that you do not interrupt social situations except in an emergency. If you have a portable phone, keep the batteries charged and do not leave it where it can get stolen.

82

CHECKLIST

1 Don't be afraid to use modern technology to reduce your time on the phone and organise your calls.
2 Only have one handset on your desk.
3 Investigate systems of call control.
4 Use machines, but no more than you need.

5 Combine machines where possible.

6 Don't have a computer on your desk unless you use it often for work as well as faxes or electronic mail.

7 Check your answering machine messages regularly.

8 Don't let your mobile phone batteries run down.

9 Don't use pagers or mobile phones in social situations.

10 Don't use machines as an excuse to make more calls than you need.

83

Organising out the hassle

It is surprising how many busy executives seem to think that working in chaos is efficient. They surround their telephone with paper (or even hide it underneath!) or else they submerge it in piles of junk. They give excuses such as – I know where everything is; it is creative; it will take too long to tidy up.

In fact, chaos on a desk indicates an untidy mind. You need to get to your phone quickly and without having to move from your chair or hunt under paper. A cluttered desk makes using the phone much more difficult and inefficient.

But with a little thought you can easily turn your desk into an efficient and comfortable-to-use workstation and make using the phone a pleasant part of your day to day routine. Don't forget to encourage your staff and colleagues to reorganise their own workstations too.

This chapter will explain how to create your own efficient and comfortable telephone workstation, how to design your own telephone note pad, and how to make sure you have access to all relevant phone numbers. Take a good look at your present workstation. Rearrange it by following the tips in this chapter to keep yourself well organised when using the phone.

Create your own telephone workstation

Before you can use your phone to the best advantage you have to be able to get at it and any peripheral machinery. You also have to have space for extra tasks connected with using the phone such as note-taking. By reordering your desk you can change your way of working for the better and make a more user-friendly environment.

ARE YOU COMFORTABLE?

An efficient workstation is a comfortable workstation. It is no good being able to get at your telephone if you hurt your back every time you reach for it or you cannot sit to talk in comfort.

Your first task is to make sure that your furniture is the right height. You should be able to sit with your back straight and your thighs supported along their length with your feet flat on the floor. Office swivel chairs are not always as good as they might be for safety or comfort. Although they are adjustable the back can slip or the seat can slip down to a lower height. Find yourself a good solid chair with a cushion if your office chair is uncomfortable.

Make sure your desk is not too high so that your arms have to bend upwards when reaching for the phone, writing or using a keyboard. If you can't lower your desk, raise the height of your chair or use a cushion – bearing in mind the height of the chair for comfort. You may need to add a foot rest for comfort.

85

It is possible to buy arm rests so that people using a computer keyboard can support their arms at the most comfortable angle for typing. If you have a keyboard on your desk or your staff use them regularly then it is sensible to consider this. It will help reduce the risk of RSI (Repetitive Strain Injury).

If possible, be near a window that you can open for fresh air. Perhaps your office has air conditioning and this isn't possible. If so, try to get outside for a few minutes at lunchtime. This will revive you and clear your head. Air-conditioning can be uncomfortably hot or cold.

It should go without saying that your desk should be well-lit and that your phone should not be sitting in direct sunlight and getting hot. Gripping an over-warm phone is no joke. If lack of light is a problem, it may be possible to move your desk slightly to get advantage of what light there is.

If sunlight is falling directly on your desk then move your desk or pull down your window blind. In some modern offices where this is not possible, a screen of large *living* plants will filter light to a softer hue.

Ideally light should fall from behind you over the shoulder of your non-writing arm so that it falls unimpeded on to your desk without subjecting you to glare.

Noise levels can be very high in some offices, especially those where managers and staff work in open-plan areas. Try if possible to get situated in one of the quieter spots. If yours is an open-plan office which uses screens to partition off work areas, ask if you can have some extra ones. If you have enough, try doubling them up to deaden the sound. If the noise is too loud at certain times to make phone calls easy to make then consider making your calls and arranging to receive them at quieter times of the day. If you have your own office, keep your door shut when you need quiet to phone.

Dress comfortably and as befits your station. It is no good looking smart if your suit jacket is so tight that you find it difficult to reach for your phone. Be careful of very loose clothing as well because this can get caught on phone handsets or in copier and fax machines. Make sure the clothes you wear will not cause you difficulty as you work.

Now that you are physically comfortable and your desk and chair are properly adjusted, you can consider how to improve the efficiency of your work space for telephoning.

86

SPACE TO WRITE

Whenever you make or receive a call you should make notes. You need room for your call sheet if you are making the call or your phone pad if you are receiving a call. You need pens and pencils to hand and plenty of spare paper. Your diary is a vital tool as well so that you can check immediately about available dates.

All these things need space. Take a simple plan of action and reorganise your work station.

(i)   Remove everything from your desk and put it on the floor.

(ii)   Pick up each piece of paper in turn and either:

- bin it;
- file it;
- act on it; or
- pass it on.

(iii) Put all other papers in one single tray at the back of your desk.

(iv)   Pick up all pens, pencils, rubbers, paper clips etc and put them in a desk tidy (if you haven't got one, get one).

(v)   Put clean paper in a drawer.

(vi) Put a clean note pad, your call sheets and phone pad at the front of your desk. Put your desk tidy near it on whatever side you write on.

(vii) Pick up each desk 'object' and decide whether you really need it. Do you really need a teddy bear shaped mug or an executive toy?

If you follow this plan you should have an uncluttered desk – can you see your phone now? – and plenty of space for making notes. What next?

WHICH EAR DO YOU USE?

The next job is to put your phone in the most convenient place on your desk. The chances are that you have not changed the phone's position since you were first allocated the desk. It has sat in much the same position ever since. You may not even have realised how inconvenient its position is. Think about it – do you have to:

- Reach across the desk to answer the phone?
- Twist in your chair to answer the phone?
- Get someone else to reach over to answer it?
- Get up from your desk to answer it?
- Change the receiver from hand to hand before it is comfortable?

87

You may do one or all of these things but none of them is necessary. First of all, decide which ear you like to use when you pick up the receiver. Do you have better hearing in one ear rather than the other? Does using one ear simply feel more natural and comfortable? Then it makes sense to put the phone on the same side of the desk as the ear you use. Make sure you place it close to your writing paper and pens.

When you have put the phone there, you may discover that you have to use a different hand to pick the phone up with. This will come naturally after a while and the change will be much easier than having to change the receiver to a different ear each time.

Zack Goldring, Business Editor of *Chemist & Druggist*, has his own theory about where to place a phone:

I keep the phone in the middle of the desk, at the back, so that I can answer it with either hand. On the whole, I use my left hand so that I can make notes with my right, but sometimes I need to grab it quickly when I've got (say) a cup of coffee in my left hand and so the phone needs to be within reach of my right hand too.

Effective listening

You may like to consider the nature of your phone conversation. We use different sides of our brains for different purposes. The left hand side of our brain deals with logical thinking and is affected by what we hear with the right ear. What we hear with the left ear affects the right side of our brain which deals with intuition and imagination. So if you have to listen to and analyse a lot of detailed facts over the phone, you might consider putting the receiver to your right ear. Alternatively, if you want to respond to your callers in a sympathetic way you might listen to them with your left ear. This technique will increase your ability to listen more effectively to people who phone you.

PIN BOARD FOR TELEPHONE NOTES

The easiest way to make sure that you do not lose telephone notes is to fasten them to a pin board. You may think that writing them down or remembering to pass them on will suffice, but it won't. You may write the notes safely on a piece of paper or on your telephone sheet but you may not remember to look at it. Or you may forget to pass on a phone message or take action after a phone call because you have forgotten the gist of it.

A pin board is a cheap and effective way of making sure that phone messages get passed on or acted on. Make sure the board is large enough to contain several messages and that there are enough pins fastened into the board for use. Many's the time a pin board has failed in its purpose because there were no spare pins to hand.

Position the board at eye level or just above on a wall to the side or in front of your desk. You may need to move your desk to make sure that you can see the board easily without craning your neck or turning around in your chair. Ideally it should be straight in your view whenever you sit down at your desk. Putting the board on the wall behind you will not do because you will not automatically see it whenever you look up and you will have to turn in your chair to pin on notes or read them. If something is difficult people are less likely to do it.

Keep a supply of A5 paper headed *telephone message*. Any smaller and the message will be too small to read at a distance or will not contain enough space for a longer message. You should not need to keep more than half a dozen messages on the board because by following the techniques in the previous chapter for organising your telephone time and acting on calls you will be constantly acting on the phone messages. Phone messages for your board could include:

- messages to pass on
- reminders about looking at a more detailed description of the call on your phone call sheet
- action to be taken after a call
- reminders to call someone back at a certain time or on a certain date.

Make sure that you record all your messages in blue or black ink and that you write them large enough so that you can read them clearly from your desk without getting up.

Every morning and afternoon when you come into work make it a priority to look at the telephone message board and act on as many of the phone messages as possible. When you have acted on as many as possible take them down to leave space for the new ones.

When you come into the office after any break take a look at the board to see whether you need to phone someone at a certain time.

Train other people who answer your phone, such as your secretary or colleagues, to pin any phone messages to the board. In that way nothing gets overlooked. Your secretary should have her own message board for calls that she must act on or pass on to you.

Properly used a telephone pin board can act as a great time-saver.

89

The ideal telephone note pad

We have already discussed a telephone call sheet which prepares you for making calls. But all efficient telephone users need telephone pads to jot down details of calls made to them. A properly designed telephone note pad will ensure that notes on loose bits of paper do not get lost or mislaid and that the meanings of the notes are clear.

Below I show a sample design for a telephone note pad. You may want to adapt this for your own organisation or design your own.

TELEPHONE MESSAGE FOR _____

OF _____ DEPARTMENT

DATE _____ TIME _____

MESSAGE TAKEN BY _____

YOUR CALLER WAS _____

OF _____

PHONE NO _____

MESSAGE _____

_____

_____

_____

_____

URGENT ☐   CALL BACK ☐   WILL CALL BACK ☐

Fig. 6.1 Telephone note pad

HOW TO DESIGN YOUR OWN TELEPHONE NOTE PAD

When recording telephone messages you will need to make sure that you have spaces for the following information:

- date
- time
- person who received the call
- person who the call is for (if someone different)
- department which the call is for
- who the call is from
- phone number of caller
- organisation of caller
- heading – main reason for call
- message
- space for initials of supervisor (if a junior takes the call)
- action to take (if any).

This may seem a lot of information to try and get on a note pad but it is important that anyone taking a call records *all* useful information at the time. Otherwise it may be necessary to phone back for more information and so waste not only your time, but the caller's. This will not give a good impression of the efficiency of your organisation.

Each of the information spaces is there for a reason.

Date and time

An undated telephone note is no use at all. There is no way of telling whether the message is urgent or is already too late to act on it. Nor does it provide a check if someone queries whether the call was received on a certain day. *Always* date your phone notes.

A similar reason applies to putting the *time* of the call on the phone note pad.

Person who received the call

The person who received the phone call may not be the person for whom the call is meant. If that person is not available to take the call then it is important to know who took the message in case there is any query about the message. The ability to talk to the person who took the call may save having to phone the original caller.

Person the call is for

You may think that passing the note on straight away will mean that you do not need to write down who the call is for. But delays happen and you may need to make queries. Always write the name of the person who should receive the telephone note together with their department – for the same reason.

Who call is from

You and I know that people often take messages and then forget to tell you who was calling. The message itself may be clear but who you are to contact may not be. Always write down the name of the caller and their phone number. There is nothing more frustrating than being unable to phone someone back because no-one knows their number or thought to ask for it.

Heading

It is helpful to put a heading such as 'Widget order' on the note so that the nature of the note is immediately obvious. Then the person receiving the note can decide whether to pass the message on to another department or act on it personally.

Message

Your organisation should train everyone who needs to answer a phone to take messages in full sentences, not note form. What may be perfectly clear in note form to the person who wrote it may be nonsense to the person who receives the note. Write all names in capital letters. Always query a name if you are not sure of the spelling.

There is a standard telephone alphabet which you can use for spelling-out names when you phone someone or for checking the difference in letters when someone phones you. It is sometimes difficult to make out whether, for example, someone is saying a B or a D. But by saying 'Is that B for Benjamin or D for David?' you can get the spelling correct. I show the telephone alphabet below:

A	Alfred	J	Jack	S	Samuel
B	Benjamin	K	King	T	Tommy
C	Charlie	L	London	U	Uncle
D	David	M	Mary	V	Victor
E	Edward	N	Nellie	W	William
F	Frederick	O	Oliver	X	X-ray
G	George	P	Peter	Y	Yellow
H	Harry	Q	Queen	Z	Zebra
I	Isaac	R	Robert		

Make sure that you take down (and say) telephone numbers correctly too. Pronounce or query them as follows:

0	OH	6	SIX
1	WUN	7	SEV-EN
2	TOO	8	ATE
3	THR'REE (roll the R)	9	NINE
4	FOER (long 'oe')		
5	FIFE		

Say each figure separately, e.g. 12 is ONE – TWO. For numbers between 100 and 900 say 'ONE HUNDRED' etc. For numbers between 1000 and 9000 say 'ONE THOUSAND' etc. When reading out a phone number break the numbers into pairs from the right and pause between pairs. For example, 435 would be 4,35 and said FOUR – THREE FIVE. 5678 would be 56,78 and said FIVE SIX – SEVEN EIGHT. If you have two numbers the same you can say, 'double three', but not if it is separated by a pause, e.g. 23–35.

If you are not the person the call is for, you may need to get someone higher up in the organisation to initial the message to show that you have completed the call.

ACTION

If during the phone call you receive a clear message about any proposed action, then you should note this separately on the note pad. If necessary, repeat this separately from the main message section. For example, it may be that someone asks you 'To phone Mr Jones tomorrow before 3 pm' or to 'confirm Octopus Holdings' order by fax immediately'. Make sure you note clearly any course of action requested.

When designing your own note pad make sure that it is a reasonable size. There is nothing more irritating than trying to record a message on a piece of paper that is too small. Anything smaller than A5 will be too cramped.

Make sure that you leave plenty of space for the message and action sections and that there is room in the other sections to record the necessary information.

Do not use a line pad as this will meant that either people will write on such a small scale that the message is unreadable or else use writing too large to get all the message on the sheet. Most people can adjust their writing to a sensible size on an unlined pad. It also looks less cluttered.

The name of your organisation should appear on the top of the note pad. This is not just for show, but so that if someone does take the message out of the office (which they shouldn't) then someone can return it to the right place. If your department is large enough you may want to include your department name as well together with your section phone number.

94

HOW TO MAKE SURE IT GETS USED

Keep your note pad on your desk near your phone along with your call sheets. As with the call sheets, make sure that pencils and pens are to hand in a desk tidy so that there is no excuse for failing to take a message.

HOW TO GET OTHER PEOPLE TO USE IT

Make sure that everyone who will answer your phone also has copies of the phone pad and that you place the pads in convenient places. It may help to have a spot of colour such as a red logo on the note pad so that it catches the eye. If you stick a similar logo to the phone then people will make the connection and use the pad.

Across the top of your telephone pin board you could keep a permanent notice saying 'Use the phone pad' so that anyone (including you) who sits at your desk to answer the phone will see it.

USING A WALL CHART

If you have regular phone calls to make at the same time each week or month you need to find a way of ensuring that you do not forget to make them. If you receive regular calls you need to be in to take them.

You can, of course, write the details in your diary. But occasionally, even in the best regulated office, you or your secretary may forget to look in it and you may not make those calls.

One way round this is to use a wall chart. Buy one large enough to be seen easily when you are sitting at your desk and pin it where you will see it every time you come into your office. Get one with spaces large enough in which to write details of several phone calls in handwriting large enough to be seen from clearly a short distance.

By putting the chart in a prominent place you will ensure that you see the calls you have to make each day. It will also help you fit other calls round them.

95

You can colour-code your calls to make it easier to plan. For example, you can write all your regular outgoing calls in red and incoming calls in green. Try to buy a wipeable chart so that if callers change the time of their regular call you can alter it on the chart without having to buy a new one.

Your secretary could have her own wall chart for regular calls to be made on your behalf.

Easy access to all phone numbers

You do not want to have to go hunting around for phone numbers when you need to make a call. Although you cannot keep every possible number in a notebook or on a telephone programmer, you should keep enough to make everyday phoning easy and have quick access to other numbers.

FREQUENTLY-USED NUMBERS

You will probably keep frequently-used numbers on your telephone programmer. This cannot accommodate all the numbers you will need during your working week. Where you have a phone or answer machine that can record many numbers, it will not show all numbers that you can write by using the keys and so you will still have to remember them.

Also, although you may know who Bob and Mr J are, anyone else who uses your phone will not. So if you ask someone else to look after the phone for you, you must leave them with sensible access to your phone numbers.

The answer is to write your phone numbers down, either in a phone number book which stays permanently on your desk or in a card file. If you use a card file you can then divide the numbers under various useful headings such as 'Internal', 'Department X', 'Firms' etc. Writing the numbers down means that you will not lose the numbers if the battery fails on the telephone or the phone is cut off. You can simply take your book and use another phone. Zack Goldring says:

> *I keep a very thorough phone book. If I learn someone's secretary's name, it goes down so that I can ask for her by name if her boss is out, or if it is something she can do for me without disturbing him. Sometimes you need to check something really basic, like how to spell their name or what their official job title is, and if you have all ready interviewed 'em it is far less embarrassing to ask the secretary.*

Most large organisations issue internal phone directories. If you have one of these check that all the information is up-to-date. It should include everyone's name, title, phone number, extension number and department. However, as these directories are not updated as often as they should be, you should ask for an updated edition every few months. If there are gaps in the directory ask for the information to fill in the gaps.

If nobody issues you with an internal directory, ask your organisation to provide one. If they will not, then it is worth compiling (or getting your secretary to compile) your own. Issue a copy to everyone in your department (don't forget to include your phone number and that of your secretary). Keep a copy in your drawer and pin one to your telephone pin board.

Also keep a list available of external numbers that are commonly used by many people in your organisation. Some people keep their phone numbers on their computer. This is only useful for them personally and only then if the computer remains on all the time. Of course, a computer cannot provide you with phone numbers once you leave your office. If someone who doesn't understand your computer program needs to use your phone list then they will have difficulty.

There do exist small computers which are basically electronic diaries and notebooks and these could contain your phone list. But generally speaking most people find that it is actually quicker to look in a phone book or in their own phone/address book.

RARELY USED NUMBERS

Keep rarely used numbers in a special telephone book marked 'Phone numbers – extra' or something similar. You will also need in your office, preferably in a central bookcase accessible to everyone, the following general directories:

- local alphabetical phone directory (residential and business where these are split)
- classified trade directories, e.g. Yellow pages, Thompson's
- telephone dialling codes booklets
- BT International Guide
- world atlas
- telex directories
- fax directory
- complete set of BT directories (if necessary for your business – these are now available on microfiche or compact disks)

You can, of course, phone British Telecom's directory enquiries if you have a name but no number. Unfortunately, this service now costs a sizeable amount of money for each enquiry. It is cheaper to find the number yourself. With the above books and directories you should be able to find any number you need.

PERSONAL AND CONFIDENTIAL NUMBERS

Any number that is personal or confidential you should not, of course, leave where anyone can get hold of it. You should not be using the office phone for personal calls but it may be unavoidable if there is an emergency. In a similar way do not encourage people to phone you at work unless it is very important. Not only will you waste time and increase the office phone bill (which will not please your employers) but you will give an aura of inefficiency to other people. You should be leading by example.

97

You should keep personal phone numbers in your own telephone book of a size small enough to be kept in your jacket pocket or handbag where it should stay permanently. Keep confidential numbers in the same book or a similar one which can be locked in the drawer of your desk. If you cannot secure your desk or think you might lose the key then you must keep confidential phone numbers with you.

But remember that confidential means just that. Do not give these numbers to anyone who is not entitled to know them and that includes friends or relatives – even your partner. If you abuse the confidentiality of these numbers then your organisation may lose business, be open to unwarranted comment or be involved in legal complications.

It follows that if you need to leave your handbag somewhere or take your jacket off then you should only do so if you can stay with it or leave it in a secure place such as a locker which can be fastened close.

EMERGENCY NUMBERS

You must keep emergency numbers where you and anyone else can find them quickly. Pinned to your telephone pin board and the office notice board is ideal with another copy in your drawer and given to all staff.

Print the numbers clearly on white card and cover them with a plastic sheet for durability. Even emergency numbers can change and so you should check these and update them every six months. The numbers must include:

- fire/ambulance/police – in emergency phone 999
- local police
- local fire brigade
- nearest hospital with casualty department
- nearest doctor or internal number of company doctor
- in relevant areas: coastguard; cave or mountain rescue; lifeboat
- water board
- plumber
- electricity board
- electrician
- taxi rank or recommended cab firm
- enquiries
- firm or department health and safety officer
- internal security.

Make sure that the sheet is headed in large letters 'Emergency numbers' so that it is immediately visible. Double-check the numbers before the sheet goes up so that there is no delay in an emergency while someone tries to find the correct number.

INTERNATIONAL NUMBERS

You can dial most countries directly on the International Direct Dialling (IDD) system. Use the BT International Telephone Guide to help you. Write down the complete number before you start and then dial steadily. Do not be put off by different-sounding tones; these vary from British tones. Be prepared to wait to be connected and so do not put the phone down until you are absolutely sure you have not got through.

Remember the difference in time zones when you make an international call. You may have to time your calls earlier or later than you would normally do in order to catch your colleagues actually in their offices.

99

Summary

You can only use the telephone on your desk efficiently if your personal workstation is well-organised and you can work in sufficient peace. Start by reducing noise by screening your desk, moving it or shutting your door if you have your own room. Try to get your staff and colleagues to reorganise their own workstations, too, to improve the efficiency of the whole department.

Spend a morning clearing your desk from clutter and rearranging your office furniture into a more comfortable position. Make sure that your desk and chair are the right height for comfort and support and use a foot rest if necessary. Ask for arm supports if using your keyboard is uncomfortable. Move your desk into good light. If the light is too harsh pull down the window blind or make a screen from living plants.

Only keep the minimum of equipment on your desk. Keep it clear for using the phone and writing. Ask yourself – do I need any machine other than a telephone?

Put your telephone where you can reach it easily and where you automatically put it to the correct ear for effective listening. Keep notes and messages easily visible on a wall pinboard.

Design and use telephone note pads. Make them large enough for clarity and include date and time of call, person receiving and sending it, room for the message and details of any action to be taken. Make sure that you have the note pads and pens always to hand. Remember to speak clearly when using the phone and spell out difficult words.

Make sure everyone has sufficient phone note pads and writing equipment to hand and that they are trained to use them for *every* call.

Keep much-used phone numbers readily available and emergency numbers in full view at all times. Keep a detailed phone number notebook and add any extra details which may help you. If you have not got a departmental or inter-office phone book them ask for one or compile your own. Keep rarely used numbers in their own book or file. Do not give out confidential numbers and keep them in a secure place. When dialling an international number take your time and do not be put off by different tones.

100

The few hours taken to reorganise your telephone workstation more than repays you by increasing your efficiency.

CHECKLIST

1 Make your workstation comfortable.

2 Make space on your desk.

3 Put your phone where you can reach it easily.

4 Listen effectively.

5 Design and use phone note pads.

6 Always check spellings of names and unusual words.

7 Speak clearly.

8 If you haven't heard properly, ask the caller to repeat what they said.

9 Store phone numbers carefully.

10 Keep emergency phone numbers easily available.

Organising calls

In previous chapters we have looked at how to control incoming and outgoing calls. You have learnt how to talk on the phone when *you* want to and how to free your time for more important work. We have described the modern technology available to help you control your calls and how to create an efficient telephone workstation.

However, knowing what to say on the phone and when to say it, or how to limit your incoming calls, is not the end of the story. You must learn how to organise your calls so that you get the maximum results for your time and so you can get on with other things.

This is not difficult to do, it just needs some planning. In this chapter I will tell you how to organise both incoming and outgoing calls so that you can increase your telephone efficiency and maximise the usefulness of the calls. I will tell you how to prepare for your calls in advance to save time and how to ensure that here are no interruptions. I will give tips on how to keep your callers' full attention. Later in the chapter I will give you an action plan to follow so that in one day you can transform your phone habits. I also will show you how one London Council arranged to improve their telephone responses with monitoring and training.

Don't take the full call now

When you receive a phone call out of the blue, do not think that you need to do everything at that time. You may be busy or you may not have all the information you need to hand. By trying to complete everything in that one call you are wasting time. Don't waste time on the phone if you don't have to. Take brief details and promise a swift reply. You will have to return the call when you have found answers to your callers' questions or have relevant information ready.

ASSESS THE CALL

When someone phones you the first thing you must do is assess whether you should answer the call then or whether you would do better to phone back later. You may need to phone back if:

- you are in the middle of an important conversation
- you are in the middle of some important work
- you are taking a phone call on another line
- you cannot answer the caller's questions
- you have not got the relevant information to hand
- you are in a meeting (really!)
- an emergency crops up with which you must deal.

In any of these situations it is only sensible to say to your caller 'Sorry, I'm in a meeting' (or haven't got the relevant papers, or whatever), 'May I call you back in ten minutes?' Make a note of when you agreed to call back and do so.

PREPARATION

It is easy for incoming calls that you have not expected to put you off your guard. Your mind may go blank or else you may give partial answers that will produce wrong results without the full facts available. Prepare for these unexpected calls by being clear what you should do about them.

ADVANCE WORK

When you receive a call that needs further research, don't be afraid to say 'I'll call you back later'. Then prepare for the call you will make. It is better to do this than pretend you know the answers and look foolish when other people discover the gaps in your knowledge.

There are a number of things you must do between the first call and your return call:

(i) **Find whatever information you need.** Take the time and trouble to gather all the necessary information. Have more than you need so that you do not have to make another return call.

(ii) **Get questions answered.** If you need to answer questions go and ask them of the people who know. Don't guess. It is important that you can give succinct and accurate answers to your caller. If you don't understand something, ask for a simple explanation. If you don't understand it, your caller won't. Don't forget to write the answers down!

(iii) **Anticipate questions.** Don't limit your questions to the ones your caller has already asked. Try to think what other questions will be likely. You can usually work out fairly accurately what possible questions you need to answer.

(iv) **Have the information to hand.** When you call back it is no good having done all the necessary research and then leaving half of it in the boardroom or on your colleague's desk. Make sure that *all* the information is to hand when you call back.

(v) **Make a note of important points.**

(vi) **Underline** particular bits in the paperwork that you need to draw your caller's attention to.

(vii) **Make lists.** Make sure you have a list of people with phone numbers and addresses which you may need to give to your caller

(viii) **Keep your diary handy.**

(ix) **Have phone sheets ready.** Make sure you have filled in a call sheet and have a telephone note pad and pens handy.

103

Once you have assembled any necessary information then you can phone your caller back and have your discussion. You will save time because you will not have to say 'I haven't got that information with me at the moment'.

All this may seem time-consuming but you will waste more time if you have to keep making calls back to gather small bits of information. By following these guidelines you will ensure that your phone calls are always relevant and that you do not waste time guessing information.

MAKE WARNING CALLS

Whether you are providing the information or need it yourself, make a brief warning call so that you both have the relevant information and documents to hand when you call back. This is means that you will both have everything you need in one place while having the phone conversation and saves you both time.

Arrange a convenient time to speak when you call back. It is no good stating firmly 'I'll ring you back at two' when the other person will be in a meeting then. Arrange a mutually acceptable time for you both to talk when colleagues are not likely to interrupt you.

If you need to fax or post each other information or plans first then make sure that you arrange to call back at a time when the information will certainly have been received and absorbed.

If you need to do this, agree on a time limit for sending material so that you can call each other if it doesn't arrive.

When you are ready to make the full call follow the checklist above so that you have everything to hand and know what major points you need to make.

If there is a deadline to meet, do not call back just beforehand so that there is no time for any last minute changes. If you are not sure what deadline you are both working to, check before you arrange to call back. Leave as much time as possible before the deadline so that you leave time for any return calls you might each need to make to finalise arrangements.

Other ways to organise calls

Before you phone back decide whether you could send some or all of the information by letter or fax. As I have said in a previous chapter, it may be more efficient to send information by other means than the telephone.

If you think it would be helpful for your caller to have the same information as you in front of him then you should fax or post the information to him so that you can both discuss it and have time to absorb it.

Linda Phipps, Divisional Retail Manager for British Rail North, has devised her own call-back action plan to save her spending hours on the phone with incoming or outgoing calls:

> 'Each day I take home a list of calls I have not had time to respond to or where the person is unavailable or number engaged. If I judge that the call can in fact be responded to by someone else I 'delegate the call' – for example, to my secretary, or to one of my team. If I need to ensure follow-through action is taken I log the call with an 'outstanding' sequence number, for example 9301 = year 1993, leaving space to check a response is received.

For each call she receives, Linda Phipps makes a note of the problem. At the end of the day she lists call-backs on a numbered list with details of the reply her secretary (or she) needs to make (see Fig. 7.1). She adds outgoing calls she needs to make to the list. These are each allocated a call sheet so that when the call is made a separate the reply or action taken is noted for the files.

The next day her secretary makes the calls using the list as a guide and notes the results on the individual call sheets (see Fig. 7.2). Each call sheet can be related back to its individual number on the list so that the reason and outcome of the call can be checked.

The saving in time is obvious because Linda does not have to spend a long time either on incoming or outgoing calls and she can note every important detail of a call.

You can devise your own system based on this and use it for calls you make and receive yourself as well as those dealt with by somebody else.

Ensuring no interruptions and full attention

We all wish that the office day was free of interruptions and that everyone you spoke to, on the phone or not, gave you their full attention. Unfortunately, life isn't like that, and so we have to take steps to make sure our phone calls are undisturbed and our callers attentive.

NO INTERRUPTIONS

If only we could lock the door and keep everyone out of our way until our phone calls are over. Only a few people have this kind of control over their office environment. Not everyone has a secretary to guard the door and field calls. So how can you make and receive your calls in relative peace and quiet?

Nobody can guarantee a time free from interruptions. After all, there may be a fire in the building or your senior manager may demand your presence *at once*. But here are a few tips for a relatively peaceful phone call:

- **Lock your door.** If you can do this, you are lucky. But you may get people banging on it if they know you are inside.

	TO	DATE	CONCERNING	RESPONSE
930370	JB	23/3	Quality Council – item on Retail Quality Improvement	*
930371	SB JS	23/3	GP–Phil. Go/Z T000S Safety Validation 6 Nov.	
930372	CAB	23/3	Phone contacts – BTP for childline	
930373	Di.	23/3	letter to Wilsons re refer on ch search MK ex. in	
939374	MC	19/3	No update on Northeast 'after TT' by Retail	
930375	DH KT	23/3	Reply to Mrs IM Keele 20 points re Surrey	
930376	JS	24/3	Rep reports to RMG of Retail Studies & Trg. Gp	
930377	TOM	24/3	NRG 'committed to the customer' – QC?	X
930378	TT	23/3	O/S, info (LIR trains) for seasons compensation calc.	
930379	GR	23/3	Proposals Action C. footpath to High St. bus stop	
930380	BILL	24/3	Alison O/C for SC. b/4?	
930381	JS/SB	23/3	re DW's comments on letter to M & SE	
930382	DM TT	25/3	Distribution list for NE (spl to this notice), NCC	
930383	KC/GR	23/3	Pls. confirm have no record vehicle retax (23/3)	
930384	KT	25/3	Reply to CK re complaints info. Watford line	
930385	D Man	26/3	KT's letter aft. repasting g. theft to Pinstille sizer	
930386	GAB	26/3	Cust. Exe. award to Steve Caldwell R02(S)	
930387	BR+MF	26/3	Schedule JDS implementing:/WS? (Nick H. 23/3)	
930388	DM	26/3	Dog handlers permits in van	
930389	SB/FS	26/3	Our regrets for env. awarness trg. rails (BS5750)	
930390	FS-JB	26/3	Update on progress + implement? GOB	
930391	FS Val	26/3	CC TV/theft Berks/BTP – update for reply Chris	
930392	A/Val	26/3	VR list (persons)	
930393	SB	26/3	All. to Red Star Staff 18.4.92 N'thern Star. – TR 25/3	
930394	CJ/BR	26/3	Reminder – 13 00 hrs. for IL (again)	
930,395	MC	26/3	Steve Capewell (& Cauldwell) to – utilise merger	

Fig. 7.1 Linda Phipps' telephone calls sheet

To: Diane

From:

**Divisional Retail Manager
North Division**

**Floor 6
Melton House
Watford**

**Ext: 00 47772
Fax: 00 47774**

My Ref: 930 360

Re: "committed to the customer"

107

> Please ring John Conway, John Thompson & Steve Gibbs
> to invite them to a meeting to exchange comment "best
> practices" on empowerment of local staff, and way
> forward, next Monday, at conference room.

LINDA PHIPPS
DIVISIONAL RETAIL MANAGER NORTH

Fig. 7.2 Linda Phipps' call sheet in use

- **Choose a quiet time.** Early morning or late in the day are good times. So is lunchtime if everyone else goes to the canteen.
- **Put a notice on the door saying 'Keep out'.** This may work some of the time. Many people will ignore it just for the sake of it.
- **Ask your secretary to guard your door.** This works well if your secretary is fierce. Some people may pull rank and ignore her.
- **Turn other machines off.** Turn off any faxes, computers or other telephones. If you are in a busy office, this is not possible.
- **Phone from someone else's office.** Only do this with their permission, otherwise you will not be popular. Of course, you may get interrupted by *their* visitors.
- **Use a mobile phone.** If you are desperate you could take your mobile phone to a quiet place (such as the caretaker's room?!) or even out of the building.
- **Use a pay phone.** Only if you are desperate. Very few pay phones in or out of offices are situated somewhere free from noise or passers-by.
- **Phone from the boardroom.** Many conference rooms are empty for large parts of the day. If you have access to one of these you will have a lot of peace – and plenty of space!

By phoning at a time when your listener has said he or she will be undisturbed at his or her end of the line you will ensure that you do not get interrupted during your call. Ask your secretary to refuse admittance to anyone during the call except in a real emergency. If necessary, lock your door. If you are in a room full of other people, turn your back on them when on the phone. You could even resort to putting a stand-up notice on your desk saying **'On the phone – do not disturb'**, although this may encourage less sensitive souls deliberately to try to interrupt you for fun.

Designate certain times of the day as 'no go' times for personal callers because that is your regular time for making long calls.

Hang a notice on your door saying **'Keep out – on phone'**. If anyone does come into your office while you are on the phone, say to the person on the phone 'excuse me a moment' then to your visitor 'come back in half an hour please'. If you have a mute button on your phone then use it. Putting your hand over the mouthpiece does *not* cut the sound out and the person on the other end of the line can hear everything being said. You need give no other explanation to anyone who interrupts you; your first consideration is to the person on the other end of the line and the person who interrupted you can see why you cannot speak to them.

One of the best ways of having uninterrupted phone conversations is to agree an unusual time with the person you are calling. If you agree to speak to each other before 8.30 am or after 6.30 pm or in the middle of a lunch hour then you stand a good chance of being undisturbed for long periods. You could try phoning senior managers on Saturday mornings. This is not as silly as it sounds. More and more senior managers are going into work at the weekend when they can catch up with their work undisturbed. If they are working in comparative peace and quiet then this is a good time to reach them with the good chance that both of you will be undisturbed. Of course, that means you will have to do a bit of work on the phone at the weekend. But if it is important enough then this may be a good way of doing it.

In an open-plan office achieving an uninterrupted phone call in peace and quiet will rarely be possible. Try turning your back on your fellow workers and retreating to the quietest corner of the room. You could call for quiet but then the whole office will listen to your conversation with bated breath. Better to leave the room and take the call elsewhere if possible.

If you share an office with one other person then you could politely ask them to leave if the call is private. This is not something you can do all the time. However, they are unlikely to interrupt you while you are phoning because they will want you to give them same consideration when they are on the phone.

KEEP THE CALLER'S ATTENTION

Once you have arranged to make a full call you have to ensure that the person you are calling gives you their full attention.

To do this, you must keep the conversation relevant and relaxed. You want to make sure that you get all your points over but that you do not bore the listener. Remember the following:

- use 'you' often so that the listener feels involved
- explain the reason for the call straight away
- give your listener time to make comments
- ask your listener's opinion
- don't phone when you are in a bad mood

- ensure that you allow plenty of time for the call
- have a note of your main points and make them clearly
- make sure that, if a course of action is needed, you both agree on it before you put the phone down.

Although your call may be strictly business, using 'you' makes the listener feel involved in the conversation and feel that his or her opinion is important. It also emphasises that the business is relevant to him or her personally as a representative of their organisation. Don't talk about 'one' because that is very pompous and off-putting, however correct it may be in certain circumstances.

HOW TO GET ATTENTION

When you speak on the phone you cannot tell what the person is doing on the other end of the line. Are they making faces at their friends? Writing a report? Tapping on their computer keyboard? Eating their sandwiches?

Because you can't tell whether they are paying attention or not you have to use tricks to make sure that they pay attention to what you are saying. Try these ploys:

- **Use 'you' frequently.** This is the most interesting word in the world to most people and invariably ensures their full attention.
- **Use first names.** If you know a first name, use it. It implies an intimacy that encourages attention.
- **Be positive.** Someone who speaks in a positive manner commands attention and encourages action.
- **Use the active voice.** Say 'We will sign the contract . . .' rather than 'The contract will be signed . . .'. The active voice sounds more 'get up and go' and encourages listeners to think likewise.
- **Listen carefully.** We have discussed power listening. Use your effective listening techniques to aim your conversation at specific points in your colleague's arguments.
- **Use the listener's key phrases.** People always think that what they say is more important than what anyone else says. So keep their attention by repeating key phrases they use in your own conversation.
- **Use star words.** These come in many guises and depend on the interest of the listener. Some common ones which usually get attention are: you, money, effective, profit, advantage and quick.

Of course, the best way to ensure attention is to make sure that what you have to say is clear, short, relevant and pleasantly said.

Action plan

Every good manager needs a telephone action plan. It can be as simple as deciding to make a few notes about daily calls in a personal telephone diary or as complicated as completely restructuring your telephone timetable and investing in modern technology to help you.

The basis of any telephone action plan must be to ensure that you and your staff have mastered the telephone techniques described in this book. You can organise this yourself but if you decide you need outside help BT can arrange in-service training or courses at national or local centres. Details of these are given in Appendix 1.

Even if you do decide to pay for extra help, you can make a start on your own. Changing a few of your telephone habits will emphasise to your colleagues and staff the importance you attach to good telephone communication. The increase in your own efficiency and effectiveness on the phone will enable you to free your time for more important work and impress your organisation and clients. If you can persuade your department or even the whole company to join in, so much the better because you can help and encourage each other. There is no reason for not starting now.

111

You have learnt how to deal with your phone calls and are putting what you have learnt into practice. But to get organised properly you need to put a day aside to prepare yourself and your office space.

If you decide that you need outside help with training, then BT can arange in-service training or courses at national and local centres. Some private commercial companies also provide training and you can get their addresses from your local Chamber of Commerce.

Even if you do decide to employ outside trainers, making a start on your own will emphasise to your colleagues and staff the importance you attach to good telephone communication.

You can work on your own, with one or two colleagues, organise your department or ask the whole company to join in. If each individual member of the company makes a start with some of the ideas in this book, they will already have a good start in learning to use the telephone more efficiently.

PREPARE FOR ACTION

Rather than tackle your phone situation piecemeal you can set aside a day to get things organised properly. Once you are prepared then you will find it easier to keep your phone under control. Try to get your colleagues to join in by reordering their phone work system. If you all change your habits, your office time-saving and efficiency should improve dramatically. Mutual support and co-operation will encourage you to stick to your improved ways.

HOW TO BEGIN

Choose a day when you know you are likely to have at least two hours of spare time and few interruptions. Start by clearing your desk of every piece of paper and equipment. Switch off and unplug all equipment and put it carefully to one side. Clean your desk – probably the first time for ages!

Now move your desk to the best position you can, ideally away from the window and direct sunlight. If you have not got a notice board or pin board on a nearby wall, put one up where you can see it easily from your seat. Otherwise move your desk.

Check the height of your chair and put a computer if you use one back on the desk and check the height of the keyboard. Put a large wastebin by your desk. When you have everything comfortable you can start putting things back.

Your phone is the priority. Bearing in mind the points in Chapter 4, place it on your desk where you can reach it easily and so that it is on whichever side that is most convenient. If you have a number memory bank on your phone, code in your most commonly-used numbers.

Now you can plug in and switch on the machines on your desk. You will probably be surprised at the amount of space you have left. Your first job is to get rid of extra paper. Be ruthless. Throw away into your large bin any paper that you don't need – last year's dinner menus, that note from Fred last month. Then pass on to colleagues any paper they can deal with. File away any important papers that you don't need immediately.

Finally, put in your in-tray only those bits of paper that you are going to act on today.

Now turn your attention to that pin board on the wall near your desk. Move it down to a level where you can see it easily when seated at your desk. Make a list of emergency numbers and pin it up. Pin your 'Check answer machine' notice where you can see it.

Now you can turn your attention to organising yourself for phone calls themselves.

Find copies of the following:

- your departmental phone list
- bomb scare forms
- call sheets
- phone listing sheets
- pens and pencils
- diary
- notebook.

113

On your desk put the writing equipment (remember that you don't need more than one pen and pencil actually *on* your desk), some call sheets and your phone log list. That's all. The less you have on your desk, the easier it will be to control your phone calls and the more space you will have for doing other work in the time you save.

Put the other things on the list into your desk drawer together with spare pens and pencils. Add your book of personal phone numbers and the bomb scare forms.

Having organised your phone space and working table, turn your attention to discovering where the extra things you need are situated.

Unless you have them in your office you need to find out where the department keeps its fax machine, photocopier and main telephone directories. When you have located them make sure that your secretary knows where they are too.

Now sit at your desk and ask yourself these questions:

- Can I see the notice board?
- Are the notices clear enough to see?
- Can I see the clock, if there is one?
- Is my phone in a sensible place?

- Can I reach my phone easily?
- Can I hear its tone and ring? (If not, adjust the ring and order a loudspeaker phone.)
- Have I got the necessary call sheets and other papers to hand?
- Do I have anything to write with?
- Have I got a list of most used numbers to hand?

If you can answer 'Yes' to all these questions then your office is organised well enough for you to make your phone calls efficiently and in comfort.

Now you need to turn your attention to how you organise the phone calls themselves. Earlier in this book we have looked at call sheets and phone call lists, phone technique and phone routine. Even if you have only been trying a few of these, now is the time to put them all into practice.

Call sheets and phone

114

It is no good having your supply of call sheets and phone call lists if you don't use them. Until you have got used to recording your calls on them automatically, consider having a card propped against your phone with **'Call sheet'** written on it. This will remind you to record your calls and will result in less lost messages.

You need to get into the habit of making a phone call list either each evening or shortly before you start work each day. This will act as a reminder of all the calls you need to make and ensure that they get done. Put them in order of priority, if you have time. Then either you or your secretary must make the calls as soon as possible in the morning and record responses and action to be taken. Just by getting into the routine of doing this will save you a lot of time.

Today, as part of your action plan, sit down and write out your reminder card and a complete list of phone calls you need to make.

If you find the design of your call sheet or phone call list unsatisfactory, now is the time to make a few changes and arrange for new blank copies to be made.

Phone technique and phone routine

The only way to get into good habits on the phone is to practice. To use your action plan to make an active change in your phone habits ask a friend or colleague to help you. Give them a list of different types of call, for example, customer compliant, wrong number, long message to take. Then ask them to ring you and answer the phone with your improved technique. Remember to sound confident and make notes. Ideally, if you can persuade a lot of your colleagues to put their own phone action plans to work on the same day, you can all help each other by making practice calls to each other.

PRACTICE MAKES PERFECT

The only way to become proficient at phone control and technique is to practise constantly what you have learnt in this book. Remember that *you* are in control. There are only four things you can do with a phone call:

(i)   ignore it

(ii) answer it

(iii) call later

(iv) pass it on.

Each of these is an important way of organising your calls.

Ignore it

If you ignore all your calls you will soon get the reputation of being unapproachable, always out and so not working, lazy or bloody-minded.

Obviously you must answer the phone, or else arrange for somebody else to do so. Whether you reply immediately to the caller or phone back later is a decision you need to make.

Answer it

You need to answer the phone within a reasonable time so that you do not keep the caller waiting. You must obtain enough information so that you can decide whether to continue with the call or to call back later, and so that you can make a reasonable stab at finding the correct information for the caller or passing them on to the most suitable person.

Call back later

You must judge from the initial call whether you can spare the time to engage the caller in conversation now or call back later at a time more convenient to yourself or when you have gathered more information.

Pass it on

If you think that the call is not within your sphere of expertise or that somebody else can answer the call more effectively, then you can pass it on. You may want to pass the call on when you are engaged in more important work. Even if you can solve the problem, you may be too busy to do so. When to pass calls on is part of your necessary action plan. These actions need to be applied to calls you make as well as those you receive. You need to spend some time constructing a secure action plan and then to apply it. If you have a secretary or colleague who regularly answers the phone for you then you need to make sure that you inform them about the plan too.

Training

Why not persuade your boss to run a 'phone improvement' day? If this was organised throughout the whole company, or even just one department or office at a time, the company's phone responses would improve dramatically very quickly.

Outside organisations, such as BT, could be brought in to provide basic technique in answering the phone if this is needed. These kinds of training sessions can be tailored to switchboard operators or management and general office staff and can be a good way of introducing staff to changed phone habits. More detailed information about training is given in Appendix 1.

Case history – Southwark Council

In 1992 Southwark Council in South London decided to overhaul its telephone system and improve its response to clients. In part this was due to the extension of facilities provided, for example, by the 071/081 split in London telephone numbers.

It also has a statutory duty as part of the Government's Citizens' Charter to achieve good telephone response targets, and, like many local councils, is working hard to achieve this. It also has to meet any targets agreed in a Borough Charter. Southwark is aiming to provide a good service to its clients. But it is aware of the need to find a middle ground between resources and expectations.

The telephone reorganisations started as a policy and this was then considered as a draft before training was implemented. It will be constantly reviewed. Southwark aims to provide a good level of service but one which has to marry what is practicable with its ideal. For example, they expect to give a reasonable level of service during their core time of 9 am to 5 pm.

There are variations in telephone service in different departments of the Council and how much they adjust depends on how practicable it is.

The Council decided that in-service training organised by an outsider was probably best because of the problem of in-house credibility. It also needed to weigh up the cost of setting up a system with a permanent trainer against the cost of staff travel and time out for training.

117

The Council called in a private company, Teleconomy, to conduct a survey of their telephone system and to organise training. The company arranged for electronic call-logging of the Council's telephone system. This recorded information such as the operators' response times and the cost of the calls, and also monitored long distance calls. Teleconomy also arranged to phone up different sections of the Council to conduct a qualitative survey.

At the same time the company provided training for operators and extension users. The particular aim was to improve users response times, salutation and the manner in which they handled calls.

The Council's aim is to increase direct dialling to at least 90 per cent, but at the moment calls can still go through the switchboard. Individual sections of the Council may eventually have their own switchboards which will be able to do almost everything that the main switchboard now does. For example, it will include a Group Pickup facility so that anyone in any one office can pick up any ringing phone and answer it.

When Teleconomy conducted its survey by phone it looked into the different response times and how the calls were handled. Certain sections of the Council were phoned up and a note was made of how many times the phone rang before it was answered. Marks were given for response time and the kind of responses given. Teleconomy issues its own awards and some Southwark operators got these. Southwark monitors its progress by comparing its own standards with other organisations. Extension users are being trained. Ideally, this should extend to the top of the hierarchy but some people rely on using their secretaries to answer their phones. But Southwark is keen that everyone should be involved in the training programme, not just the secretaries.

The Council found that there was a need to change people's attitudes to telephone training. There was initial resistance from operators; now they accept it as part of their job and wider practice. The training is now an ongoing part of their job.

The Council is aware that extension users need to be more responsible and accept telephone training as part of becoming more professional in a climate of customer awareness. They need to be motivated and should receive greater credit for improved telephone technique.

Southwark Council has specific aims for its telephone operators, relating to response time, salutation, how calls are handled and the time spent on calls.

The Council aims for a response time of four rings or 10 seconds for switchboard operators and five rings or 15 seconds for general users. A phone should not be left ringing for longer than necessary. If staff are in a meeting they should take a convenient break ('excuse me, I must take that call') and make a quick response. They are not allowed to ignore the phone and carry on. This needs a change of attitude to the phone.

As regards salutation, operators and extension users are instructed to say as much as is necessary to let the caller know how near they are to the person or section they need to speak to. In an organisation such as the Council the operator should go as far as is practicable and say 'Southwark Council' plus the Department and their name. The response should start with a greeting such as 'good morning'. Sometimes the salutation can become so much of a habit that it is spoken too quickly and unintelligibly. Operators are encouraged to speak clearly and slowly.

The question of giving personal names is a sensitive issue and one which the Council is looking into. Some areas of the Council, such as Social Services, are vulnerable to verbal and physical abuse and giving a name could leave staff open to danger.

In a general office it is not always necessary to give a name and internal phone users can choose whether to do so. Responders with their own client list will need to give their own name. This is an issue which the Council is still looking into.

When operators are handling calls, the Council expects its phone users to know how to get information or who to go to for it. No caller should be left on hold for more than 30 seconds while their query is being dealt with and someone should get back to them at intervals. Hands should not be put over the receiver nor the receiver put on the desk because the caller can hear everything.

If the call has to be transferred the next person should be given all the information so the caller doesn't have to repeat it and the recipient knows who is calling and why the transfer has been made. The person transferring the call should give the caller the new name, phone number and department so that if they get cut off they can ring the transfer number directly. If an extension user is away from the phone it is their responsibility to make sure that someone will answer it.

119

Staff are now expected to reduce the time they spend on calls and must not use the phone as an excuse to relax. Answering machines are used in some overworked sections of the Council, such as Social Services, but their use is under review elsewhere in the Council buildings.

Southwark Council would like all its phone users to achieve these standards and train in telephone use. Although it doesn't expect all its senior executives to do so it feels that they should. Ideally they would like to see telephone training for everyone with follow-up and reminder courses together with a rolling programme of training.

The code of telephone practice for the Council has been widely circulated in the council newspaper so that all local people are aware of the standards they should expect when they phone the Council. The result of the Council's telephone retraining programme is a greatly improved response time and quality of response and a more approachable and available service for local people.

Summary

Simply rearranging when you make and receive your phone calls will provide you with more work time but will not entirely solve the problem of how to improve your telephone efficiency. You must ensure that each outgoing and incoming call serves a useful purpose and that you do not waste any time when on the phone.

Planning calls is vital. If necessary, arrange to call back so that you can prepare for the call. Make sure you have all the relevant information to hand when you make the call back. When you return a call you must: have found whatever information you need, got any questions answered, anticipated questions you will be asked, got all the information to hand, made notes of important points, highlighted special points, made lists of relevant phone numbers and addresses, placed your diary to hand and made sure your phone sheets are ready.

Make warning calls to prepare the other person so that you both have all the information ready. Communicate by letter or fax if you do not need to phone.

Ensure that you are not interrupted when on the phone by either locking your door, choosing a quiet time to phone, putting a 'keep out' notice on the door, asking your secretary to guard the door, turning other machines off, phoning from somebody else's office, using a portable phone, using a pay phone or phoning from a boardroom.

To keep the other person's attention use key phrases and 'star' words such as 'you', 'money', and 'profit'. Ask the listener's opinion and give them time to make comments. This draws them into the conversation and they take more notice. Repeating the other person's phrases keeps their attention, too.

Have a telephone action plan and put it into practice as soon as possible. Either take a few hours to reorganise how you use your phone or involve the whole office. If necessary arrange for training from an outside organisation, such as BT.

First clear your desk and then rearrange your furniture. Throw away any unnecessary paper. Pin up a list of emergency numbers. Make sure that in or on your desk you have a departmental phone list, bomb scare forms, call sheets, phone listing sheets, writing equipment, your diary and a notebook. Make sure you can reach your phone easily and that everything is within easy reach.

Practise dealing with various kinds of phone calls by asking your colleagues to act the part of the caller. Remember the four things you can do with a phone call – ignore it, answer it, act on it, pass it on.

CHECKLIST

1 You don't always need to reply straight away – call back.
2 Prepare for your calls.
3 Make warning calls.
4 Have all the information to hand.
5 Keep the recipient's attention.
6 Take steps to ensure your calls do not get interrupted.
7 Choose an 'action day'.
8 Prepare your workstation.
9 Practise your phone technique with friends.
10 Arrange for official training in telephone techniques.

121

Rights and responsibilities

Some callers think that because you cannot see them at the other end of a phone line then they can get away with being rude, interrupting people with impunity and wasting people's time.

But just because you are on the phone to someone does not mean that they have the right to treat you without respect. You have rights when you are making and receiving phone calls just as if you were speaking to the other person face to face. The phone is such a potential source of irritation that it is vital that users have good phone manners.

Do not put up with rude or insensitive callers on the phone. Stand up for your rights. You will gain the respect of people whose opinion you respect and put off those who are intolerable.

In the same way, other people are entitled to be treated with respect and consideration. You have a responsibility to yourself and your organisation to treat callers as you would wish to be treated by them.

Read this chapter to find out how to ensure that your rights are respected and what is the essence of good telephone manners.

You will learn how to keep people on hold without making them angry and who should make a return call. You will find out who can be on first-name terms with and how and what kinds of greeting will cause offence.

I will discuss the problem of malicious calls and explain what to do if you receive a bomb scare call. There is information about how to complain about bad telephone manners and who to complain to. All this will make sure that your calls are treated with respect and that you do not inadvertently offend somebody else.

Phone manners

Remember that you, too, must have manners when you are on the phone to someone. Do as you would be done by. If you treat people with respect and courtesy then you have the right to expect the same treatment yourself. But if you forget your manners on the phone you have only yourself to blame if others treat you in the same way.

Remember, too, that you have a responsibility to set a good example to your staff. Often a person's only contact with your firm is by means of the telephone. You want all your clients to remember your firm with respect and pleasure because of the good service and nice manners of the person who answered the call. An off-putting phone manner by anyone from the telephonist upwards can put a person off an organisation for life. Treat your callers with respect and courtesy and make it clear to all your staff that you expect the same standards from them.

123

LANGUAGE

You may be so used to speaking on the phone that you do not recognise when your language is inappropriate. It is very easy to be lulled into a false sense of familiarity which can be off-putting to any caller.

It does not sound professional, for example, to use slang expressions such as 'Okay' or 'Hang on'. It may sound natural but will give the caller a feeling that the organisation is sloppy and casual.

In the same way you should be careful about what you say about the organisation and the individuals in it. What you say to one person over a phone line may get repeated to all their friends and acquaintances. A chance remark derogatory to the company may result in lost business or ruined reputation.

Nobody would expect you to take elocution lessons or try to hide your accent. The days are long gone when everybody had to speak the same way in business. But that is no excuse for using the language in a sloppy way. The key word is *appropriate*. In the same way that schoolchildren will speak in one way in the playground and another at home, you must remember that you should maintain a professional standard of speech at work, however you choose to talk to your friends in your leisure time.

You can be safely guided by the concept of good manners. It is good manners to make sure that you speak clearly and that your meaning can be understood. It is polite to address the caller by their name and to offer a greeting. It is good manners to treat the caller as a valued colleague rather than a casual accountancy.

All this may mean that you should speak in a slightly more formal way than you might normally. But this ensures that everyone has the same basis of understanding about the meaning and tone of what you are saying.

For people you know well within your company you may feel able to adopt a slightly more informal attitude, but you should still speak in a way that does not allow your meaning to be misunderstood.

Just as you should be polite and clear in your speech over the phone to others, you should be able expect the same standards from your callers. You should not have to put up with over-familiarity, bad language or incomprehensible speech. While you are within your rights to complain about the first two and refuse to deal to callers who speak to you in this way, in practise the third is more difficult. Someone who has a speech problem, a strong accent, a poor command of the language or perhaps is excessively shy or nervous can make it difficult to understand them. All you can do in this situation is to continue to speak well to them and try to elicit their meaning. You will need patience and a sympathetic attitude, but you would hope for that if you were in the same situation. Staff should be instructed to refrain from making rude or sarcastic comments to people who have difficulty communicating over the phone.

124

HOLDING PATTERNS

There are various ways of holding a call so that the caller does not get fed up and ring off. Choose one that is appropriate to your organisation. For example, long periods with music in a small firm simply implies that there is no-one there at all.

Do try not to keep someone on hold. It is very worrying, not to say annoying, for a caller to have to hold on to a silent line wondering whether you have forgotten them, are ignoring them or whether they have been cut off.

If you must leave your caller, perhaps to answer another phone, then say

'I have to answer a call on another line. May I phone you back?'. This means that you are giving the caller the option of holding on or waiting for you to call back. If the caller agrees that you can call him or her back, do so immediately you have completed your other call or have dealt with the emergency, or whatever took you away from the phone.

You should train your secretary or the telephonist to ask callers if they would like to hold on if you are unobtainable or busy. If they agree, and there is a long wait, your secretary should cut in every few minutes to say 'I'm sorry, Mr Jones is still engaged. Will you still hold?'. If the caller decides not to hold, then they should be asked whether they want to leave a message or be phoned back.

If finding you is a real problem your secretary should explain that, so that the caller does not feel neglected.

Some large companies have music playing while customers hold on. This can be pleasant if the caller is only on hold for a short while, but anything longer than a few minutes is unacceptable, not least because the music is usually anodyne and a short extract is repeated *ad nauseam*.

125

Such a system also seems to indicate that the customer is in for a long wait. It is much more reassuring for the caller to hear a human voice every so often. Even if your company does use music, the telephonist or your secretary should still cut in to reassure your caller.

LIMBO

It is disconcerting for you or your caller to be left in limbo with no sound at all coming from the phone. This happens when your call reaches the switchboard and is put on hold without any music, voice or sound to tell you that you have been put on hold.

Alternatively you might get through to someone who presses the mute button and keeps it on for a long time while they have a chat with somebody else.

Another occasion might be when you are in a call waiting system. You might get a sound or music for the first few minutes and then hear the sound of a switch. Then silence. You have no idea whether you should hold on or wait for somebody to answer your call in turn.

Sometimes this is just bloody-mindedness on the part of the person receiving the call and effectively you have been cut off or forgotten. Where you know you are supposed to be in a call-holding system and this happens and you get no answer in a few seconds then you can be sure that you have been cut off.

In any case your time is valuable and you cannot afford to hang on in limbo. As soon as the line goes silent wait for no more than ten seconds. If no-one answers then put the phone down. In a proper call-waiting system the phone only goes silent just before somebody answers it.

If you have a phone system that will redial until you receive an answer you can use this. However, it is best not to waste time on such people, but to try another number, write or fax. If this does happen then write to the person in charge of the firm or organisation you are calling and point out the deficiencies of their phone answering system. They may have wondered why one section hadn't received many orders recently! In any case bad manners should be dealt with.

126

WHO CALLS YOU BACK

In general, it is the person who initiates the call who should make the running about calling back, unless the person being called insists on doing so. If somebody phones you, then the caller is imposing on your time and so should be prepared to accommodate your wishes as far as is reasonable. Try to give a definite time for calling back, for example 'Please will you phone back in 10 minutes, Charles? I need to finish this work'.

If your caller reaches you when you are busy, then they should ask you when it would be a suitable time to call back. Then it is up to them to do so.

If you are having a phone conversation and get cut off, it is the person who made the call who must redial and try to get reconnected.

WHAT DO YOU CALL THE CALLER?

Even in these days of more liberal manners and socially freer mores, it is still considered impolite in Britain to address someone by their first name on first acquaintance unless you have been asked to do so. In other countries, particularly the USA, first-name terms on first meeting are the norm. But when making a call to a business in another country err on the polite side until you have found out what is acceptable. Women, in particular, seem to find it offensive to be called by their first name without warning because it smacks of condescension and the 'boss/ secretary' relationship. A first approach should be 'Mrs Charles, this is Mary Jones'. You can get onto a less formal footing later if you get to know each other better.

First names at work should work both ways unless there is a large age gap. It is arrogant of a manager to be 'Mr Harris' when his secretary remains 'Sally' or 'George' unless his secretary has made it clear that a first name is acceptable. Usually it is polite to initiate first-name terms only after several phone calls to one person.

Pet names

Lovie, ducks, mate, dear, and other informal names may seem unthreatening and even jokey, but in fact they can cause a great deal of offence.

127

Words such as these are usually the calls of street-wise men who fancy themselves on friendly terms with everyone in an 'I'm just a bit of a friendly lad' type of way. What you might put up with from a 70-year-old stall holder in the market place you may well find offensive from an executive in your company. In the latter case it smacks of condescension and treating of the other person as someone not deserving of official respect. In the case of men calling women by these names, it is a mild, albeit just as unacceptable, form of sexual abuse. Few men would address their colleagues in that way. It implies a closeness and familiarity which is not necessarily the case and hints at an intimacy which may be distressing to the woman to contemplate. The rule is – address all your colleagues and fellow workers, of whatever rank and whatever their age or sex, with decency and respect. While you can call men 'Mr' or whatever their title is, women have at least three possible forms of address – 'Miss, Mrs, Ms' or title, if any. It is annoying for women if you address them by one form if they prefer the other. Not all women wish to be called 'Ms'. Many, even in these liberated days are proud of bearing the title 'Mrs' and many a single woman prefers 'Miss'. Where a woman has kept her single name for work you should respect that. It is polite to find out how your women colleagues prefer you to address them. If you have to phone a woman in another company whom you do not know, then get your secretary to enquire how that woman wishes to be addressed. Of course, if a woman has a title such as 'Dr' then this should be used.

In fact, once people have got to know each other it is quite natural to start using first names. If you are unsure, then say 'Do call me Mary', or 'May I call you John?'. It is polite for the senior of two business colleagues to initiate first-name terms. But in most cases where you are dealing with people of equal status as yourself, then it can be up to either of you. If you feel friendly towards the other person and have spoken to them several times on the phone then it would be perfectly natural to initiate first-name terms. As you are in a business situation you may find that keeping a bit of formality between yourself and the person on the other end of the phone can be more efficient than a general mateyness. If people are too friendly in a business situation, it is tempting to delay tough decisions by drawing on the friendship as an excuse – 'Bit of a problem, Joe, you won't mind if I think about it for another couple of weeks, will you?'. This puts the other person in the difficult position of having to decide whether to deny a friend.

You will need to judge for yourself when it is sensible to keep a more formal footing and when to be more friendly, and if so by how much. In most offices colleagues and people you deal regularly with on the phone will not mind the first-name approach. Some offices and companies prefer this 'all in it together' attitude.

MALICIOUS CALLS

One of your most important rights is the right to do your work in a secure environment, free from physical and verbal abuse. Unfortunately, although modern communication systems make contact between people by phone much easier, they can also make people more vulnerable. Phone and fax numbers are widely available and anyone can pick up a phone and make a threatening or malicious call.

It is not only women who can feel threatened by this exposure by the telephone system. Staff of both sexes working in sensitive areas, such as a Social Services office, can be subjected to this kind of unpleasantness.

It is easy to dismiss malicious phone calls as simply something to be shrugged off until it happens to you. It can leave people miserable and scared and afraid to go out of doors. The feeling of being threatened in a safe place makes it worse.

This type of call should be taken seriously whether it is you, a colleague or a member of your staff who receives it. You should take prompt action to try to get the caller traced as well as take steps to erasure the person called. If that means moving them to another phone line, or getting somebody else to answer their phone for a while, then do that.

We usually think of malicious calls being received at home. But it is possible, though perhaps more unlikely in an office situation, that you may get callers who are simply abusive or foul-mouthed. Women are more likely to receive the 'dirty' phone call or heavy breather while men may come in more for simple abuse, although such divisions are certainly not strict.

A nasty phone call may even be a criminal offence. Section 3 of the Telecommunications Act of 1984 states that:

(1) A person who –
a) sends, by means of a public telecommunication system, a message or other matter that is grossly offensive or of an indecent, obscene or menacing character; or
b) sends by those means, for the purpose of causing annoyance, inconvenience or needless anxiety to another, a message that he knows to be false or persistently makes use of for that purpose of a public telecommunication system, shall be guilty of an offence and liable on summary conviction of a fine not exceeding Level 3 on the standard scale.

The official advice is to keep calm because malicious callers enjoy upsetting the person they are calling. If the call is on a domestic phone you should simply to say 'hello' and wait for the person to identify themselves. In an office situation where callers expect you to give your name this can be difficult. However, if there has been a spate of such calls, then it may be necessary to instruct staff not to give their names for a month or so until the problem has been solved.

In most cases you will know who the caller is. If someone you know suddenly becomes abusive or obscene simply say 'I'll call you back' and put the phone down. Then ask someone senior to deal with the problem. If someone who has normally been pleasant during previous calls suddenly behaves like this then there is obviously something wrong. In this case a word to your superior with a suggestion that the caller's personnel people and boss should be informed immediately will deal with the problem.

A more upsetting and potentially dangerous situation is the anonymous caller. If a caller refuses to identify him or herself immediately, refuse to talk to them. If they do give a name but the conversation becomes unpleasant later, put the phone down immediately. Some malicious callers enjoy talking so do not give them the pleasure of an argument or long chat. In both cases contact British Telecom immediately so that they can discuss how they and you can work with the police to stop the problem. Also inform your security department, telephonists and boss.

BT can help you deal with unpleasant calls and has an efficient system in place to help victims of this type of call.

BT can change your number to ex-directory although this may not be practical in an office situation. It can trace calls and co-operates with the police to catch the callers. You need to be prepared to give evidence in court if the caller is charged.

If you get one of these unpleasant calls try to note as much information as possible – background noise, male or female voice, accent, the date and time of the call and so on. If the call is left on an answer machine save the tape. Never answer irrelevant questions over the phone.

BT has a counselling service for people who have been victims of these callers.

Bomb scares

The one case when you must take a call seriously is if the caller claims to have information about a bomb planted whether in your building or elsewhere. Unfortunately, this is now a problem that everyone must take seriously. Make sure that everyone in your company from the telephonist to the boss is aware of how to handle such a call. The official police guidelines are:

(i) Immediately alert someone else if possible (so that a Senior Officer may be informed) but **do not put down the handset or cut off the conversation.**

(ii) Obtain as much information as you can.

(iii) Try to keep the caller talking (apologise for bad line, ask him to speak up, etc.).

(iv) Complete the first form (see Fig. 8.1) as you go along asking questions in sequence as necessary.

130

(v) After the call give the form to the Senior Officer who will decide what to do.

(vi) Complete the second form (see Fig. 8.2) as soon as possible.

Everyone in the company should have a copy of each of the two forms shown in their desk or somewhere close to hand so that if a bomb call comes they can start to take down information immediately. The longer you can keep the caller talking and the more information that can be gleaned, the quicker the police can reach the scene and clear the area while searching for the device. Your security will have a set procedure for evacuating the building which you must follow as soon as the call is over if you are asked to.

It is not up to you to decide whether the call is genuine or not. Do *not* make that decision yourself. Your job is to inform someone and get as much information as possible. By following this advice you may save lives, including your own.

131

DIRECT LINES AND PRIVATE NUMBERS

It is usual to be put through to someone's secretary or via the company's telephone exchange. However, it is becoming more common for managers to have a direct line. If this is the case then you will get straight through to the person you are calling with no introduction. You must try to ensure that you call at a time convenient to the other person and that you have a good reason for calling. After all, you will be interrupting another busy person's day, just as phone calls distract you from your work in hand.

Always say who you are and the name of your organisation, unless they know you well. This identifies the call as genuine. Say why you are calling too. This gives the other person a chance to say that they are busy. It is unfair to phone someone directly and to withhold your name or reason for calling.

If he or she has time to talk then, as I have said before, make your points without rambling. Offer to call back later if they need time to think about what you've said.

It is possible that you may have to phone someone at home on a private number. Again, try to choose a suitable time and identify yourself and

Immediately alert someone else if possible (so that a Senior Officer may be informed) but **DO NOT PUT DOWN THE HANDSET OR CUT OFF THE CONVERSATION.**

Obtain as much information as you can.

Try to keep the caller talking (apologise for bad line, ask him to speak up, etc.).

Complete this form as you go along asking questions in sequence as necessary.

MESSAGE (exact words) ....

....

....

....

....

....

Where is it?...

What time will it go off? ....

What does it look like? ....

What kind of bomb is it (type of explosive)? ....

....

Why are you doing this?..

Who are you? Name: ....

Address:..

....

....

Time of call ....

WHEN THE CALL HAS FINISHED GIVE THIS FORM TO THE SENIOR OFFICER WHO WILL DECIDE WHAT TO DO. THE MORE INFORMATION YOU GET, THE EASIER IT WILL BE TO DECIDE WHETHER THE WARNING WAS GENUINE OR NOT. COMPLETE THE OTHER SIDE OF THE FORM AS SOON AS PRACTICABLE.

132

Fig. 8.1 Bomb scare telephone message sheet
Reproduced with the permission of the Directorate of Public Affairs, Metropolitan Police.

DETAILS OF CALLER

Man .... Woman .... Child .... Old/Young ....

SPEECH

Intoxicated .... Rational........................... Rambling...................

Speech Impediment .... Laughing ....

Serious... Accent...

Was the message read or spontaneous?...

DISTRACTIONS

Any noise on the line? .... Call box pay
tone or coins...

Operator... Interruptions ....

Anyone in background? ....

OTHER NOISES

Traffic.................. Talk...................... Typing.................. Machinery ....

Aircraft .... Music .... Children.......................

Other ....

Person receiving call..

Number of telephone on which call was received...

Fig. 8.2 Bomb scare caller record sheet
Reproduced with the permission of the Directorate of Public Affairs, Metropolitan Police.

your organisation to whoever answers the phone – which could be anyone from the partner to the two-year-old child.

Don't ask a child to 'get Daddy or Mummy' unless you say who you are. Say 'Please tell Mummy Mr Jones from Walbrook Firm is calling'. Parents worry when their children say 'a man called but I don't know who he is'.

If you first speak to someone who is not the person you are calling be prepared to answer any reasonable questions about yourself and the nature of your call. You are after all invading someone's privacy and the wife or boyfriend may have been told 'If it's someone from X firm, I'm out' or 'If it's about Y, I must speak to them at once'. Many families get irritated by work calls to the home, however important. So never make them unless you really have to.

134

Bad treatment – how to complain

If you make a call and the recipient treats you with rudeness or abruptness, keeps you hanging on for too long, cuts you off frequently or simply doesn't answer the phone for ages, what do you do? Who do you complain to?

First decide how bad the offence was. Was it a one-off curtness from a usually helpful and cheerful member of staff? In that case, put it down to a one-off bad day and phone another time. Was it only once, but extremely unpleasant and upsetting? Then complain at once. Do you get continual rudeness and unpleasantness when phoning a company? Then complain.

TELLING TALES

It is rarely worth trying to argue with the person who is being awkward. They will simply become belligerent or more abusive or simply cut you off.

The trick is to go over their heads. Do not be afraid of telling tales on other people who treat you badly on the phone. You have a right to courteous treatment when on the phone, just as you do when face to face with someone. In fact, many of the people who are rude on the phone would not dream of treating you in the same way if you appeared in front of them.

It may simply be nerves, they may have been badly instructed in the use of the phone or they simply be bloody-minded. Whatever the reason, you don't have to put up with it. If it is a telephonist, contact the personnel department and explain your problem. The personnel department is usually in charge of organising the training of telephonists and can deal quickly with the offender. Any good organisation that values its public image (and they all ought to in these days of decreasing trade) should be horrified at the poor image of the organisation which is being given out and the implied inefficiency.

If, for some reason, they do not respond in a suitable manner, there are a number of other alternatives:

- Write to the head of the organisation
- Phone or write to your local councillors
- Write to the press.

135

If you write to any of the above people always copy your letter to all the others. This will set the cat among the pigeons and will ensure that all the telephonists are lectured on the need for customer care!

There are usually guidelines laid down for telephonists such as the maximum number of rings they may leave the phone ringing for, how to address the caller, how to deal with callers on hold. Ask the personnel department for a copy of these guidelines so that you can quote them back at the organisation concerned.

If someone's secretary is unpleasant, do tell their boss. This will usually cause great embarrassment because a person's secretary represents that person to the public and the rest of the organisation. If the person you are calling is in the same company, it is best to meet them and have a private face-to-face chat about the problem. If they are elsewhere mention it in a letter (otherwise of course you will encounter the same problem again trying to get put through!)

If you have been put through to the wrong department and the people there are rude then complain to the head of the company. Why put up with bad behaviour?

It could be that whomever you phone in a company is unco-operative. This may be lack of training in telephone skills or simple laxity in the company towards customers. Are you sure you want to deal with a company that has such a low regard for its clients? If possible, refuse to have any more to do with it and write to the head of the company explaining exactly why.

If you have to go on dealing with them, try to deal with the most responsive person available and do not forget to complaining whenever somebody treats you are badly on the phone. Encourage your colleagues to do the same if they phone the same company. Eventually it may get the message.

When complaining about bad treatment on the phone remember the following:

(i) **Keep calm.** State your problem clearly and give details without ranting.

(ii) Try to **find out the name** of the person who is being unco-operative.

(iii) **Make a note of the facts**. Record the name of person who was rude, time, date, and how they offended you.

(iv) **Write a letter.** If you will have to go through the same person again, put your complaint in writing.

(v) **Contact someone higher up.** The letter then goes down from the top – much more effective than the other way round.

(vi) **Don't be afraid to tell tales**. You will be doing the company a service.

What should you do if someone complains to you about your secretary, telephonist or colleague? If it is the telephonist, go to your personnel department. If it is your secretary, call him or her in and have a chat with them about the job. Explain what the problem is. Then go through carefully with them about how you like your phone answered. Some secretaries are simply unaware that their bosses expect them to answer the phone in a certain way. Explain that they represent you. Praise their other work if possible. But make it clear that you expect good telephone behaviour.

If, as occasionally happens, a secretary does not respond properly to this encouragement to do better then you seriously have to consider changing them. Your reputation and the reputation of the company are at stake. Can you afford to have your clients put off?

A colleague who answers your phone and is rude or unco-operative is a different matter. You could ask them not to answer your phone or try saying 'You rather upset old so-and so when he phoned on Tuesday'. But if you think that this is unlikely to be met with consideration then you will have to approach your boss. If it only happened occasionally – and which of us doesn't have an off-day – then it is probably best to leave it. If it is a frequent occurrence then you will have to act. Dealing with your colleague is a matter of judgement; you, after all, have to go on working with them. But if they are upsetting your clients on a regular basis then you have no alternative but to take steps to improve the situation.

Summary

The simple rule about telephone manners is 'do as you would be done by'. Treat other people with the respect you wish for yourself. Don't assume that because you can't see the person on the other end of the line that they won't mind if you are rude to them.

137

If you have to keep callers on hold don't keep them hanging on for long periods without an explanation. Do not cut them off in the queue. If this happens to you, hang up and try another time. If it happens frequently, complain to the company concerned and if necessary do not use that company again.

If a return call is needed at the end of a phone conversation, it is the person who made the call who should phone back.

Do not use informal names because they may cause real offence. Accord women the respect of using whichever title they prefer. After you have spoken to someone several times on the phone it is permissible to call them by their first names, but if in doubt, ask first.

If you receive dangerous or malicious calls contact the police and BT. Callers can be traced and the problem should be dealt with quickly. Follow the police guidelines if you receive a bomb scare call. Try to note as much information about the voice and background noise as possible as well as the message.

Don't abuse people's availability by phone. Try not to contact them at home or when they are in a social situation unless it is urgent. If you do need to phone somebody at home, explain exactly who you are.

Do not put up with bad treatment over the telephone. You are entitled to good manners from the person you are speaking to. If they continue to be ill mannered, complain to their superior. Keep a note of the facts of the unpleasantness and keep calm.

Do not be deliberately rude to anyone on the phone. Not being visible is no excuse for being unpleasant and you could ruin your own reputation and that of your company.

CHECKLIST

1 Do as you would be done by.

2 Don't keep callers in limbo.

3 Don't use offensive names.

4 Treat callers with respect.

5 Ask BT to help you deal with malicious calls.

6 Learn and follow police guidelines for bomb scare calls.

7 Do tell tales about callers who treat you badly.

8 Don't make business calls to people's homes unless the calls are urgent.

9 If you need to complain, contact someone higher up.

10 Don't allow your secretary to let you down by having bad phone manners.

Power tricks

It's your phone and you need to stay in command of it. You cannot afford to let callers or the machine itself dictate your working day. You have now learnt strategies for regulating your calls, both in and out. Now you have to ensure that you are in command when you are making or receiving a call.

If you have followed the advice in this book so far, those calls that you do make and receive will now be at a time convenient to you. You will be getting the most from your calls by careful preparation and adequate note-taking.

But now that you have restructured your day and put your phone calls in their place, you must look at how to win with your phone.

Even if you have got over an initial nervousness about the phone and are making calls when you feel at your best, there are other ways of making sure that each phone call gets you the result you want. You must not let the other person lead the conversation or decide the outcome.

Staying in command is not about getting your own way by getting angry or shouting. Getting your own way is about knowing how to use the phone effectively and which power tricks will guide the conversation the way you would like.

Your aim must be to gain something from each phone call, whether incoming or outgoing. The person on the other end of the line will be trying to do the same, but *you* must prevail. To do this you need to know what tricks to use to keep the power in your hands and how to reach the outcome you want. This chapter will remind you about the assertiveness techniques we learnt in Chapter 3 and will then show you techniques for getting the upper hand in a telephone conversation. It will show you how to keep the power in your hands when you have gained the upper hand.

You will also learn how to build up a personal power base by getting on first-name terms with callers and by networking over the phone. By reading this chapter you will learn how to make sure that it is *you* who prevail in any telephone conversation.

Remember – be assertive!

As we have seen in Chapter 3, assertiveness is not being aggressive or rude. Having a negative attitude and trying to get your way by shouting or getting angry is more likely to make your callers dig their heels in and react against you. To be assertive you need to stay calm and sound confident while making your points clearly.

Do not be overawed by the person on the other end of the line. Keep in mind the point you want to make, the reason for the call and what you want to achieve.

Do not be deflected by other matters and do not get upset if the other person is rude or aggressive. You gain nothing by being rude or getting angry.

Be non-judgemental and try to find some common ground if you have to make a difficult point. It is always better to be able to say 'I agree that we should be doing that, but we can't do this . . .'.

Keep calm, however emotional or angry the other person becomes. If you both get embroiled in an emotional scene, then the discussion with degenerate and nothing positive will be gained.

ASSERTIVENESS CHECK POINTS

- prepare for your calls
- keep your aim in mind
- be firm
- do not get upset or angry
- do not be rude
- say 'No' and mean it
- do not agree to anything you don't really want to.

Think yourself into a confident frame of mind. Remember the other person cannot see you, only hear you. So if you sound confident and speak firmly you are already more than half way to achieving your aims.

Once you have decided what you want from a particular telephone conversation, you must force the issue to get the desired outcome. This demands special techniques.

Forcing the issue

Because you cannot see the person on the other end of the telephone line and they cannot see you, you may think that the only way to force an issue and to get the phone conversation running your way is to talk loudly and aggressively. It is easy to imagine that by raising your voice or being rude you can force the issue because the other person can only respond to the sound of your voice.

But think how you react when you hear people speak like this. Doesn't it make you want to disagree with them? Don't you feel you should entrench yourself in your position instead of meeting the other person half way?

If this is how you are likely to react, then so might the person you are speaking to.

But there are other ways of guiding the conversation towards the goal you want. Read on to find out how.

SILENCE IS GOLDEN

Silence is a valuable tool when it comes to forcing the issue over the phone. It is amazing how many people cannot bear silence whether they are speaking to you face-to-face or talking to you on the phone. In this day and age when we are surrounded by continual noise silence makes many people nervous. They try to fill any silence with talk even if it is inconsequential.

Use this to get the upper hand. When someone makes a silly remark or one that you cannot answer without getting angry, just keep quiet. You may find it difficult to do this, so practise. It is very effective. The other person becomes worried and nervous and starts talking again. Often they will say things they hadn't meant to because the silence has 'forced' it out of them.

Don't forget that silence on the phone has more force than when you are face-to-face. It sounds more powerful and almost forces the other person to speak to fill the void. This can be very useful if you are negotiating on the phone. Make your points and then stay silent. The other person will feel obliged to speak and what is said and how it is said will give you a clue to their feelings and the likelihood of them agreeing with you. You can then phrase your response to react to them.

By forcing them to speak first you make them reveal their feelings. This gives you an edge in any power move.

You may remember the advertisement involving a musician who was phoned by a record company. 'We want you to play at a recording session. £100 per day.' Unfortunately the doorbell went and the musician went to answer it leaving the receiver on the floor. The silence unnerved the caller. 'Okay, £200.' Silence '£300?' By the time the musician had sent his visitor away and had returned to the phone it was only to hear the caller say 'Okay, Okay! You win. £1000 final offer!' Only then could the musician speak 'fine'.

Silence is a wonderful tool. Use it sparingly and you will find that you will win more arguments and get results from your calls.

KEEP IT SIMPLE

If you want to force the issue you must keep your line of persuasion simple. If you overwhelm someone with facts and figures, opinions and ideas, they will not be able to sort out what main points you are making. By providing them with too much information you are confusing them and diluting the force of your argument.

Decide what you want to achieve from your call and work out a few key points. For example, if you want to persuade someone to sign a contract with your company you could include in your points:

(i)   your company provides an excellent product or service

(ii) your company is cheaper than similar companies

(iii) you provide a fast and efficient service

(iv) any problems are dealt with within 24 hours.

When you have decided your points, stick to them. Make your call and make your points. Do not deviate from them. There may be other points that you could make and which may be partially relevant. But you don't need them. All you need to do is to persuade someone to do this one thing.

If the person you speak to tries to lead you into a conversation about other aspects of the problem, return the conversation to one of your main points. 'Transportation is no problem. As I have said, we offer a fast and efficient service . . .'

REPETITION

If you need to get something done, don't be afraid of becoming a 'stuck record'. Repetition works well by drumming the point into the other person – or by wearing them down! Keep repeating your main points until you have got agreement for each of them in turn. Keep calm while you are doing this. However slow someone is in understanding what you want or reaching an agreement, it is not in your interest to get angry or impatient. Be a dripping tap and steadily wear your 'opponent' down.

143

PATIENCE

It will be no help to you to get impatient during a phone call. The other person will sense your irritation and that will antagonise them. By becoming impatient you will also be more likely to lose your train of thought and so lose a grip on the way the conversation is going.

However irritating you find the other person, and however eager you are to bring the conversation to a satisfactory conclusion, do not rush things. If the other person has one more point they want to make before reaching a decision or asks you the same question again, do not get angry. Let them have their say and respond calmly to the question again. By letting them say everything they want to you are allowing them to talk themselves round to your point of view. The more you listen, the more you will learn that you can use this to persuade them when your chance to speak comes.

There is nothing to be gained by rushing somebody into a decision. If you make them move too fast they may decide that their original decision is the one they will keep. A few more minutes and you may have talked them round to your point of view.

STAND TALL

To sound more authoritative on the phone, try standing up to phone. The person on the other end of the line cannot see you, but you will give yourself a feeling of superiority and this will give you confidence while pressing your points. By standing up you are literally heightening your sense of authority, rather as some interviewers make sure that they have higher chairs than their interviewees.

LEAN BACK

You will feel more in command of the situation if you are relaxed. It is very easy to hunch up in your chair while using the phone. This in turn clenches your muscles and you feel tense.

One way of overcoming this is to lean back in your chair. If you have the standard office chair you will not be able to lean back far, but your body will straighten and allow you to breath more deeply. Be careful not to push the chair backwards – if you fall off, you will certainly find it difficult to sound decisive and in command!

When you have straightened up or leant back take a few deep breaths to relax you. Most people do not use all of their lungs when breathing and take shallow breaths. Take long deep breaths to fill your lungs and engender a spirit of well-being.

Once you feel calm and relaxed then you will feel better able to cope with even the most difficult of phone calls.

YOU DECIDE FIRST

When you need a decision and you want to force the pace, you will do best to ask for a decision before the other person gets round to doing so. By making it clear that you want a result you are putting the onus on them to come to a conclusion. It is in people's nature to agree rather than disagree, if possible, so by making them decide then and there. Under pressure they are more likely to give you the answer you want.

BE POSITIVE

Don't say anything that could be construed as hesitation on your part. Be positive in your statements and when you think that you are both

144

near reaching a decision you can say firmly 'So we'll do that then' or 'So you'll sign the contract tomorrow – will 2.30 do?'. It will be difficult for the other person to disagree, especially if they have been making positive responses to your proposals.

PHONE FIRST

Power comes in making the first move to put your opposite number at a disadvantage. In terms of using the phone that means making that important decision-making call first.

By calling first you have decide to take up the other person's time and by accepting the call they agree to this. You can then expect to take the lead in any conversation and you can direct the conversation the way you want it to go. The other side of this coin is that whoever starts a phone call can best end it without causing offence. This gives you the ideal opportunity to make a decision making statement and then end the call. This not only gives you the upper hand but saves you time because you dictate the length of the call.

145

SIDESTEP THE PHONE

One useful power trick is to sidestep the phone altogether. If you know that someone in your own organisation is expecting a phone call from you, put them off guard by calling round. They will not have had time to prepare their speech and will be taken aback to have to talk to you face-to-face. Some people prefer to work by phone calls only because it makes *them* feel powerful. By going to see them in person, you gain the upper hand.

BE DEVIOUS WITH DIFFICULT SUBJECTS

Sometimes the best way to deal with a difficult subject, is, as I have said elsewhere, to get straight to the point. But although this can be effective on most occasions, there may be some subjects that would immediately get a negative reaction if brought into the conversation too early. 'Would you like early retirement?' springs to mind as a subject that many people would give an immediate 'No' to without some thought.

In this case you need to bring the subject up while talking on another issue. Wait until you have to phone the person about another subject which they feel more positive about and then introduce your subject after a suitable interval. 'By the way, I also wanted to have a bit of a chat about . . .'

DON'T HESITATE

No decision will go your way if you prevaricate. If your conversation is going well but you hesitate when asked for details, it will lose momentum. Make sure that you have any important facts and figures to hand so that you can sound confident when asked for particular points. But remember what I first said and don't use too many. One or two important facts are helpful, a bookful is not.

OFFER ALTERNATIVES

It is possible that you will need definite dates from the conversation, but you expect refusal or at best hesitation. Be prepared and have several alternative dates to offer. Say 'If Tuesday at three doesn't suit you, what about Wednesday at five or Friday at 10?' It will take a lot of excuses for anyone to sound convincing about being unable to accommodate even *one* of your proffered dates. Once you have an agreement for a date, confirm it and then put it in writing.

POWER LISTENING

Most people do not listen carefully. They hear the words but do not really take in what they mean. It is important that you practise the art of power listening if you are to keep control of any telephone conversation.

Get into the habit of listening carefully to pick up any hidden points from the talker. Can you tell from what they say that they are really nervous or unsure of themselves? Does the way they phrase sentences make it seem as if they do not really agree with what they have been told to say? Are they blustering without enough solid facts to back up their argument?

Listen carefully and say as little as possible until you are clear about what they are *really* trying to say. Then you can adapt your arguments to them.

Although you should not say much at first, encourage the other person to speak with the occasional supportive phrase such as 'I see . . .' or 'I understand . . .'. Be careful that you do not use these so often as to be irritating.

Don't do anything else while listening. You cannot concentrate properly if you are writing a report or drinking a cup of tea. Don't interrupt while the other person is speaking, even if you don't understand their argument. Listen first and then use your important main points to change their mind. Make notes, if necessary, to fix the main points clearly in your mind. By listening powerfully, you may be able to use the other person's own words in support of your own arguments. For example, if they say 'Donald is worried about how this contract may effect our foreign suppliers' you can counter this by using the same phrase: 'I understand why Donald is concerned about the effect on foreign suppliers. He is sensible to be aware of this. We have solved this by . . .'. Tone of voice can convey a lot if you listen carefully. The speaker may be saying one thing but their tone of voice may indicate quite another attitude towards it. You can use this conflict to your advantage by playing on their ambivalence to what they are saying.

147

Listen for any jokes, however slight. This often indicates the covering up of nerves or embarrassment. If you realise that this is the case then you have them at your advantage. Check that what you *think* you heard is actually what you did hear. We all get into the habit of expecting to hear certain things in certain contexts. For example, we may always expect our mother-in-law to say 'Yes, dear, I can baby-sit on Tuesday evening' and not take in the fact one week that she says 'Yes, dear, but I can't baby-sit on Tuesday evening'. This can pave the way to embarrassing misunderstandings.

By making good use of power listening you can make sure that any such misunderstandings are someone else's problem.

Get it in writing

Keep the upper hand by confirming decisions in writing as soon as possible after any phone call. Don't wait for the other person to do so. If you write first then you can phrase the letter to your advantage. Subtle turns of phrase can make all the difference when drafting decisions. Having made the first move on to paper you are the one who is consulted first about any changes.

If it is important to get the decision on paper quickly then use your fax to send confirmation. Use a letter if time is not so important but still remember to get your letter in first.

Use your phone call to establish that you are going to write the decision down and make it seem as if you are in control of all subsequent paperwork.

However agreeable the conversation, however positive the response, nothing is final until you get it written down or officially confirmed. A good technique for forcing a positive conclusion is to say firmly at an appropriate point 'I'll confirm that in writing then'. A brief 'good-bye' after this will bring the conversation to a close. Make sure that you confirm the decisions in writing as soon as possible, so that you do not allow enough time for anyone to ponder too long on the subject. If you give them too much time to do so, they may pluck up their courage and reverse the decision. By putting the decision in writing you are trans-forming the nebulous world of the spoken word to the more formal and permanent expression of the written or printed word. Something on paper gives an immediate feeling of permanence and works very much to your advantage. Don't wait for someone to say it to you during a phone conversation otherwise you might find that you are the one faced with the permanent paper and someone else's decision.

Getting a decision in writing also has a more practical point. Although decisions can be made and contracts agreed over the phone, it can be difficult to enforce them unless there is also a permanent record of the agreement. This means that if you reach an agreement with somebody over the phone and they then fail to honour it, you may have difficulty making them keep their word or even proving that the agreement took place. Or perhaps they may keep part of the agreement but alter details.

So it is in your own interests to make sure that any agreement reached is confirmed in writing as soon as possible. That means that if there is any disagreement, you can assert your rights with success.

Do not be led by the supposed intimacy that talking on the phone can give you. A phone conversation where first-name terms are used and conducted in a friendly spirit can lull you into forgetting that any important decisions must be confirmed in writing. If you think you might forget, warn your secretary or a colleague that you are about to make an important phone call and get them to ask you afterwards 'Did you reach a decision? Do you want it confirmed in writing?'. Don't rely on the person you are calling to draft a written version of the decision. As I have said elsewhere in this chapter, if you draft it, you can phrase it to satisfy yourself.

First-name terms

I have already discussed in Chapter 7 the rights and wrongs of using first-name terms. But, assuming that there is no real reason why you should not be on first-name terms with the person on the other end of the phone, how do you use the phone to get to that stage?

Some people simply call people by their first name on the phone right from the start. That puts the onus on the other person to say 'I'd prefer to be called Mrs Smith', which is not as easy to do as you might think. It makes you feel as if you are being unfriendly or impolite. That may be necessary or expedient if you wish to maintain a slight distance in a working relationship.

Obviously the correct and polite thing to do is to say, perhaps on the second or third call, 'May I call you Peter?' and wait for confirmation. Most people will agree if they feel that they have had some previous contact with you over the phone.

Zack Goldring, Business Editor of *Chemist & Druggist*, admits that getting on first-name terms helps him establish that he is of equal status with the person on the other end of the line. He says:

> *It's just a psychological trick. Salesmen do the same thing, but to establish a sense of intimacy and trust. However, you can't be too crass; I find it often better not to use first-name terms 'til the second time you speak to someone, then when I get put through I'll say 'is that Mr Smith? Hello Jeff, it's Zack Goldring of* Chemist & Druggist . . .' *Having said that, I very rarely 'Mr Smith' someone all the time, unless they seem exceptionally stuffy.*

Another way to get on first-name terms is to write to the person you want to call and sign it with just your first name. If you get a reply in similar terms and/or they address you in their reply by your first name then it is a simple matter to assume you have the right to do so on the phone.

You can often judge whether first-name terms will be acceptable by listening carefully to how the other person conducts their phone conversation. If they sound cheerful and make the occasional joke then you will probably be safe in calling them by their first name.

As manners are more relaxed nowadays and we copy more from our American friends then first-name terms are becoming more common over the phone as everywhere else. Most phone callers simply assume first-name terms after one or two calls or even a few minutes on the phone and continue in that vein unless firmly rebuffed. So on the whole if you want to get on first-name terms over the phone then you are safe going ahead.

If you feel nervous about it then try these tricks:

- Pretend someone has interrupted you and say casually 'Hold on a minute, John, someone's just come in'. By the time you get back to the conversation you will have established first-name terms.
- When the other person says 'This is Sally Martin' say 'Is that Sally or Sarah?'
- Reverse of the above – when you get put through to someone say' I'm trying to get through to Charles, or is it Charlie Harrap.' The reply will be something like 'Speaking and it's Charlie'.
- Ask for someone by their full name, not Mr or Ms, so 'May I speak to Betty Noaks please?'

While all these tricks may be useful there is no real polite substitute for asking. Because you are on the phone in a business capacity the other person will be more likely to feel friendly towards you and allow you this privilege.

PERSONAL DETAILS ARE POWER DETAILS

Sometimes during a phone call you will glean snippets of personal information about the person you are speaking to. Perhaps they will mention the name of their wife or children or perhaps their favourite restaurant.

Make brief notes of these during the call and immediately after the call transfer them to a diary or card index under the name of the person you spoke to.

Personal details like this can pave the way for future co-operation from people who might otherwise be impersonal or unfriendly. The fact that you can ask after their wife by name or that you remembered that little Johnny passed his clarinet exam puts your relationship on a more personal note.

Do not overdo this. A brief reference to a personal detail is enough, then get on with your business. You just need to establish that you are someone who has their interests in mind.

NETWORKING

A further step on from simply noting personal details and occasionally dropping them into the conversation is the game of **networking**. This, as everyone now knows, is the art of getting to know people who may be useful to you in your job. There may be many reasons why you would find networking helpful. You may

- want information about a new product
- want off-the-record information about personnel
- need a recommended contact
- need a reaction to a new proposal
- want an expert view on a particular subject
- want inside information about a new job!
- need an outsider's view of a company event
- want to be recommended for a new post

151

or any number of other reasons. Networking gives you the chance to get information without going through official channels. It keeps you up with opinions and news which might not reach you until too late to be useful and it makes sure that your name is kept in the minds of people who may be useful to you. Of course, you in turn may be useful to them. You do not need to have met someone to be able to judge from what they say and by the way that they say it whether they are trustworthy or competent. When you have talked to someone about work related matters on several occasions and perhaps exchanged a few social details you are in a position use them. Being on first-name terms and being able to indulge in a brief social exchange establishes them as part of your personal network. This means that they are more likely to respond to your request for help or offer of work.

In the same way, of course, they will judge you by your conversation and manner so it is in your interests to listen carefully and speak responsibly.

Once you have several telephone contacts, do not be afraid of asking them to recommend other contacts. This is how networking progresses. If you can telephone a stranger and say 'Hello, is that John Brown? My name is Barry Green. Sally Waner told me you are the best person to talk to about management technology' then you are well on the way to making another long-term contact.

Good networking never stops. It just expands in different directions.

Summary

Your phone can make you powerful. By sounding confident and planning your calls you already have an edge over most phone users. Add to this the power tricks to help you make the first move and also power listening and you are already a force to be reckoned with.

Stand up to make yourself feel more powerful and confident or if you need to relax, lean back in your chair. You will then sound relaxed and in command on the phone.

Do not be scared of using silence as a power tool. Most people find silence unnerving and it will force them to speak first to fill the gap.

Do not make your points too complicated. If you want to force the argument your way a simple approach is best. Keep repeating your points. Give yourself confidence by standing up – remember the other person can't see you.

When a decision needs to be made, get your version in first. That way you can decide how it gets put into action. If you need to raise a difficult subject, don't give the other person a chance to react in a negative way. Raise the subject when you are talking about something else.

To get the other person off guard, make the first call. Try phoning them directly instead of through their secretary or calling round. Listen carefully to what the other person is really saying and adapt your conversation accordingly.

Get any decision in writing quickly.

Get on first-name terms with as many contacts as possible. Make notes of any personal details you learn and mention them occasionally. Network as much as possible. Ask for other phone contacts, to recommend you to other people.

CHECKLIST

1 Be assertive on the phone.

2 Force the issue by using power tricks.

3 Use cold-calling techniques.

4 Listen carefully – hear what's *really* said.

5 Use repetition and keep your points simple.

6 Make the first call.

7 Be the first to put it in writing.

8 Get on first-name terms.

9 Make a note of callers' personal details.

10 Network, network, network.

Technology glossary

■

Increase your phone efficiency by using modern technology wherever possible. As long as you don't let machines become time-wasting toys they can increase your power over the phone and increase the time you can spend on more constructive work. Here is a brief guide to who does what in British telecommunications, followed by a glossary of technical terms you may come across.

Who does what?

BT, formerly British Telecom, no longer has a monopoly of the whole telephone network. The 1984 Telecommunications Act now governs the way the telecommunications system is run in this country. Enforcing the legal requirements of this Act is largely the responsibility of the Director General of Telecommunications at OFTEL. Private firms can compete with BT to sell equipment, such as telephones, for use with the telecommunications system. This means that users can, if they wish, buy instead of rent the equipment. Business users can buy or lease equipment.

Technical standards for equipment are set for the EC by The European Telecommunications Standards Institute and these are translated into national standards by the DTI and approved by the Secretary of State for Trade and Industry. They are then written by OFTEL. These standards are checked by the British Approvals Board and other smaller companies who test new procedures and equipment to make sure that they comply with the agreed standards.

It is illegal to run a public or private telecommunications system without a licence and these licences are issued by the Department of Trade and Industry (DTI) by the Secretary of State. The Telecommunications and Posts Division of the DTI advises the Secretary of State which licences can be issued to applicants.

The Office of Telecommunications (OFTEL) monitors the system and processes applications for private licences which are passed to the DTI.

The Secretary of State can licence private sector firms to provide independent telecommunications services as well as equipment. This includes leasing part of the BT network to provide telephone services at profit to third parties. BT itself can licence private sector organisations.

There are three licensed fixed-link public communications operators (PTOs) in the UK. These are BT, Mercury Communications Ltd and Kingston Communications (Hull) plc. Three other operators have been granted temporary licenses for providing one-way Europe-wide satellite communications systems.

BT (Formerly British Telecom)

BT has to provide a universal telecommunications service, a service in rural areas, and essential services such as public phone boxes and emergency services.

155

Mercury Communications Ltd

This is owned by Cable & Wireless, Barclays and BP. Users can access the Mercury system by buying a phone with a Mercury button which they press before making a call to be billed to Mercury. Each user has a code for their phone so that bills can be debited correctly. At present about 80 per cent of the country can use Mercury.

Mercury is licensed to provide national and international public telecommunications services for residential and business customers. These use the digital network created by Mercury. It can also provide public and private telephone services, national and international telex, international packet data services, electronic messaging, data network services, and customer equipment.

Private telephone services

There are more than 260 private telephone companies which offer information on a variety of subjects. Some use the BT network, others the Mercury network. Companies using BT lines must ensure their services adhere to the codes of practice in the Independent Committee for the Supervision of Standards of Telephone Information Practice.

Mobile phone systems

Two companies are licensed to provide competing cellular telephone systems. These are Cellnet, jointly owned by BT and Securicor, and Racal Vodaphone Ltd, owned by Racal Electronics Group. Another company, Hutchison Telecom, provides Rabbit phones which can only be used within 100 yards of a Rabbit communication point.

Customer-installed phones

Customers can install telephone extension sockets and apparatus on their own premises. But they must have a master socket which can only be supplied and fitted by a public telecommunications operator (PTO). Customers do not have to buy or rent their phone equipment from a PTO but the equipment bought from a retail outlet must be of a standard approved for use with the public network.

<u>156</u>   What this means is that there is now more competition to provide you with a variety of phone equipment at competitive prices either for sale or rent. To start making choices you need to know what the equipment does: so read the following glossary.

Technology and terms

The following list will provide you with an overall understanding of the latest phone technology and telecommunications terms.

Abbreviated dialling

Most electronic phones will store numbers and these are activated by use of a short code number of two to four digits. A computer controlled exchange can be programmed to dial numbers automatically when two or three digits are dialled.

Absent extension dialling

If an incoming call to an extension gets no answer within several rings then it can be transferred or re-routed to a pre-arranged extension. If there is no answer from that extension then the process is repeated.

Acoustic coupler

This device converts electric pulses from a key operated machine into sound in the form of acoustic waves. The sound can then be transmitted or received along telephone lines to and from computer terminals. Computers can connect like this by using a modem and a telephone handset.

Answering machine

A machine which records on tape telephone messages. On most models the owner can leave a message for callers. It can be combined with a telephone and a fax machine.

ASR (Automatic Send and Receive)

A teletypewriter and receiver enables calls to be automatically sent or received when used in conjunction with a typewriter.

157

Audio standby

By this means you can leave the *Talk/Receive* button on cordless phones on *Talk* when you replace the handset on the base so you can receive calls just by lifting the handset.

Automatic call-back

Incoming calls switched to an extension which does not receive an answer in a specified time can be made to re-route automatically back to the operator for attention.

Automatic dialling device

This is a term for such devices as the BT Callmaker series which stores telephone numbers chosen by the operator for assisted dialling.

Automatic last-number redial

On certain phones you can press one button to redial the last number called automatically if that number is engaged or there was no response.

Automated telephone line address system

A storage bank where operators store programmed numbers for calls to be made later. The operator programmes STD or IDD codes into the storage bank and these can then be automatically redialled by pressing a button on the console.

Automatic transfer

On some extensions the user can dial a code and then the extension number they want and be transferred automatically without going through the switchboard.

Broadcasting

The ability to send a fax to many destinations at once.

158

Call-barring

A system which enables you to bar the use of certain areas of a telephone system such as STD (Subscriber Trunk Dialling) or IDD (International Direct Dialling). It means that an extension can be barred from making unauthorised calls, and in some cases from receiving incoming calls.

Call counter

A visual indicator on an answering machine which shows you how many calls you have received.

Call diversion

Incoming calls to one extension can automatically diverted to another selected extension. The telephone system can be programmed to do this when the first extension is busy or for all calls to that extension.

Call forwarding

Transferring callers from anywhere in the country to a local number which automatically intercepts their call and transfers it to wherever your phones are situated.

Call indicator

A flashing light on a phone which shows that it is ringing.

Call logging

A system of monitoring telephone traffic and recording information about calls made and received, usually on a printed sheet. It records the numbers dialled and the extensions making the calls. Phone users can automatically charge all relevant calls made their behalf to particular client accounts. A record can be kept of all outgoing calls from each extension with the length of the call and the numbers dialled. A print-out can be obtained.

Callmaker

A device which is used with a telephone to input numbers in a simple one or two digit dialling code. Some have in-built loudspeakers and most have the facility to repeat the last number dialled.

159

Call metering

A device fitted to the telephone console records the units used for each extension on a PABX system. Calls can then be charged to individual accounts (see 'call-logging').

Call screening

A means of choosing which calls you want to answer.

Call-sequencing

A system using a machine which answers calls from more than one incoming line and holds them in sequence until someone is ready to deal with them.

Call (speech) amplification switch

A way of boosting your caller's voice or your own over the phone.

Call transfer

Calls are transferred to another extension.

Call waiting (call holding)

If a caller phones you and you are engaged they will hear a message asking them to hold on. You will hear a bleep to let you know that somebody else is on the line. You can put the original call on hold and speak to the second caller or switch back and forth between the two.

Card Callmaker

A BT Callmaker which uses a punched card to store and dial numbers.

Car phone (mobile phone)

A phone which is fixed in a car and can be used there. You can buy a kit to enable you to use your car phone as a portable phone.

Card phone

A public phone which accepts a telephone card instead of money. The card records a certain number of pre-paid units which are then deducted as the call is made.

Cellnet

The BT and Securicor cellular network within which mobile phones can work. This now covers 98 per cent of the population.

Central control unit (CCU)

The electronic brain of the phone system which is usually stored in a compact, wall-mounted box.

Changed identity re-routing

Night service numbers which are different to day-time extension numbers. Callers can get through if they know someone's night service number.

Channel selection

A system on mobile phones which enables you to switch channels if one channel has interference.

Charge advice service

Formerly known as ADC (Advice of Duration and Charge), this is a BT service which enables the telephone operator to meter the call and provide details of the cost. There is a fee payable as well as the cost of the call.

Chargecard

A card which enables you to make calls from any phone and charge the calls to your own business or home.

161

Circuit (line) switching

Individual circuits are interconnected to form a continuous connection via successive exchanges. Therefore transmission is possible to each circuit directly.

Conference call

Up to seven parties can be connected by an extension user or operator.

Console

The keyboard of an electronic switchboard.

Cordless phone

A portable phone which can take or make calls within 100 metres of the base unit. The base unit has to be a fixed telephone with a line. It can be used as a two-way intercom between the base unit and the handset.

Datel®

Short for **Data** and **Tele**communications. A system where data from one computer terminal can be sent to another. It passes through a central computer where the data is processed and made available on demand. The data is converted to a form suitable for transmission by a modem. Users connect a modem to their telephones to enable the data to be transmitted to them.

BT leases circuits to enable data to be transmitted over the telephone network. There are various types according to the speed of transmission.

Digital voice prompt

A message on an answering machine which prompts the caller to leave a message.

Direct dialling in

If users know the direct dialling number of a telephone extension they can dial direct without going through the switchboard. This facility is available on PABX systems.

Electronic mail (e-Mail)

A means of sending information via the phone or by other means using a digital system.

Electronic switching system

This is a digital telephone system which provides special services such as speed dialling, call transfer and three-way dialling.

Extension

A telephone line connected to the same incoming line.

Extension group hunting

Extensions are arranged in groups. Incoming calls are routed from phone to phone in a specified extension group until answered. This can sometimes be done on internal phone systems.

Fax (facsimile machine)

A machine which transmits and receives documents over a telephone line. It copies documents electronically and sends them down a phone line to a similar machine which automatically prints out an exact copy of the document. Both the receiving and transmitting fax machine must be compatible. According to the type of machine it can use thermal or plain paper and will print either by heat, laser or ink-jet systems. It can be combined with an answering machine and a phone. By adding suitable hardware and software to computers it is possible to transmit (fax) documents directly from a computer via phone lines to another computer.

Freefone®

This is a BT facility available by means of the telephone network. Companies are given a Freefone® telephone number. Customers dial this number and are connected to the company at no cost to themselves. The company is charged for the call and is charged a fee for the facility.

GRACE (Group Routing And Changing Equipment)

A system which enables charges to be made for calls via STD.

Group 3 compatibility

An international set of standards which most fax machines need comply with before they can communicate with other fax machines.

Group 4 compatibility

A new set of international standards for fax machines.

Hands-free phone

A phone which enables you to take and make calls without lifting the receiver.

Headset working

Where the handset can be replaced by a headset.

Inductive coupler

A handset which helps people with hearing aids with a 'T' position switch hear more clearly.

Integrated Services Digital Network (ISDN)

A network carrying digital information which can combine speech and data in the same channels and so provide a wide range of faster and better quality communications. Present equipment can be used by linking it to a terminal adapter and so to an ISDN line.

Interactive video

Information sent from a computer to a recipient by cable and usually by means of telephone lines. Users can react with the computer. An example is Prestel®.

164

Intercom

A device which lets communication occur between two or more places without the need to go via the main telephone system or switchboard.

Key system working

Where a system is set up so that incoming calls can be answered at every extension.

Last number redial

Press a button on the phone to redial the last number called automatically.

Line box

The modern box attached to an incoming telephone line into which telephones are plugged.

Liquid crystal display (LCD)

A display panel showing the number being called and/or other information such as the time and date.

Local Area network (LAN)

A system which links computers, e-mail, word processors and other electronic office equipment to form an inter-office network. A network can be given access to external networks such as the public telephone system.

Mail box

Mail system by which a message on one user's computer can be transferred to the file of another user's computer.

Master socket

The main connecting box bringing an outside line or lines into a building and from which the inside lines run. This must only be connected by a BT engineer.

165

Message pager

A pager which shows the message on a screen.

Message switching facility

A device on a telephone exchange which lights up if a connection is attempted but not answered. It shows the user that a message is waiting.

Messaging

A means of letting extension users know that a message has been left for them in their absence.

Mixed mode dialling

This allows for dialling in both pulse and tone mode during the same call.

Mobile phone

The familiar name for a car, portable or transportable phone which can be used anywhere within a geographical cell. They can either be two-way battery operated radio phones which operate in a closed circuit or the new cellular phones which have a wider area of coverage. The phones run on batteries and usually have a message screen too. You can buy a kit to let you use your portable phone as a hands-free car phone.

Mobile phone interface

A device to let you receive or transmit data within the cellular network. It connects directly to your mobile phone and links it to your fax or laptop computer with modem.

Modem

This is short for **Mo**dular/**Dem**odulator. It is a device which converts digital signals from computers into electrical waves which can then be transmitted along standard telephone lines. When the signal is received it is converted back into digital signals by a similar device at the receiving end. The information is usually sent by e-mail or fax.

<u>166</u>

Multiplexer

This device controls the traffic of data and/or phone calls over a private line or circuit. It enables many users to connect their desktop terminals to a single line without causing jams.

Mute button

A button on some telephones which when kept depressed allows you to speak and not be heard by the caller.

Night busying

A PABX switchboard can operate on selected extensions only. After close of business, incoming calls can be automatically transferred to particular extensions by setting engaged signals on extensions which are not needed.

Night service switchboard

A limited switchboard service for night time. Calls are automatically re-routed from the main switchboard to a smaller switchboard which may be manned by a security officer. Incoming calls are limited.

On-hook dialling

This allows you to dial a number without lifting the handset until someone answers.

Operator

Person who operates a switchboard or telephone system.

Optical fibre (Fibre optics)

Very fine flexible pure glass thread able to carry 1000 times the information possible with copper wire. It is bundled together as cable. It allows telecommunications to occur by means of passing pulsing light from sources such as lasers and light emitting diodes down these bundles.

167

Overdrive

Certain callers can be allowed to break into another person's phone conversation.

PABX (Private Automatic Branch Exchange)

This system lets users dial outgoing calls directly from their extension without the help of the switchboard operator. An external line is chosen by dialling one number and then the external call can be made direct. Incoming calls are handled by the operator and internal calls are dialled direct.

Packet switching

A means of routing data from transmitter to receiver by splitting a message into small packets. The split is carried out at the transmitter terminal or exchange and each packet contains the address of the message's destination. At the receiving end the packets have to be sorted and reassembled. In *autonomous* mode each packet is sent individually within the network to the address. In *virtual link* mode the packets follow a particular address route once the route has been decided.

Pager

A small radio receiver which fits in a pocket. It is activated from a central control board. The recipient hears the signal which tells him or her that they are being 'paged' and so must contact the central control board.

Parking calls

Switchboard operators connected to the telephone network may 'park' a call if an extension is engaged to an incoming call. The call is held in store for the operator but is connected when the busy extension is free.

Pause facility

This is for use when you want to store numbers on a phone connected to a switchboard where you have to dial an access number to get an outside line.

Payphone

A public or private phone which is operated by putting coins into it. It can be operated at the standard BT rate or, on one model, you can set your own charges.

PBX (Private Branch Exchange)

An internal telephone system which is not connected to the public telephone network. It is used for interdepartmental communication and leaves outside lines free for incoming calls.

Phone base

Direct access to BT's Phone Book database through a computer link for businesses which use directory enquiries between 20 and 300 times per week.

Phone disk

A monthly updated compact disc holding all of the UK's listed phone customers, except those with ex-directory numbers. This is available for firms which make more than 300 directory enquiry calls each week.

Pick-up group

A group of extensions where any user can answer a call by bringing it from another extension to his own.

PMBX (Private Manual Branch Exchange)

All incoming and outgoing calls are routed via the switchboard operator. It allows the operator to monitor outgoing calls. Internal calls are usually operated on a separate system.

Prestel®

A public viewdata system by BT using the public telephone system. Prestel® transmits text, pictures and diagrams from a central computer onto a television screen and so provides a public information service. It can be used by anyone who has a specially adapted television set and a telephone.

169

Private circuits

Exclusive lines connecting two points at home or abroad. These are usually used by different offices in the same organisation.

Private lines

Lines set up by individuals, either domestic lines for the owner's own use or private commercial lines operated within specified geographical restrictions.

Prompt

If you phone an engaged number the phone stores the number and bleeps three minutes later to remind you to try again.

PSTN (Public Switched Telephone Network)

The means of interconnecting users via telephone exchanges in order to distribute computer data over a wide area network. It is carried out by telephone exchanges but is also used by others for special purposes, i.e. circuit switching, message switching, and packet switching.

PTO (Public Telecommunications Operator)

Company licensed to provide fixed-link public telecommunications services.

Public viewdata

System for sending and receiving information to a screen, such as a television screen, to anyone who has the right equipment, for example, BT's Prestel®. It is run on a subscription basis.

Rabbit phone

A cordless phone which can be used within 100 metres of specified public base unit phones.

REN (Ring Equivalence Number)

A number which enables you to work out how many phones can be connected to your exchange line. Each piece of equipment has a REN. The maximum REN capacity of each exchange line is four.

Ringer column control

This control allows you to adjust how loudly the phone rings.

Saved number redial

This stores numbers given during a call for redialling later.

Security code

A number used to prevent callers getting remote access to your answering machine. On cordless phones it stops your number being used by anyone else with a similar phone.

Serial calling

A person who wants to speak to more than one person can be automatically returned to the operator for connection to the next number when the first person hangs up.

Speaker volume control

For adjusting the sound level of the loudspeaker on phones you can use hands-free.

Speech volume control

A way to increase the volume of your own or your caller's voice when using the speech amplification switch.

STD (Subscriber Trunk Dialling)

Direct dialling to a distant location by use of a telephone code.

Stored number redial

This stores numbers in a phone so that they can be redialled by pressing one or two buttons.

171

Switchboard

An external telephone installation connected to a telephone exchange. It is possible for a switchboard to have more than one exchange line and many internal extensions. Calls can be manually or automatically connected to the right phone. Most PABX systems are electronic and have no moving parts.

Systemphone

A phone which has been designed to take advantage of a particular phone system.

System X

BT is replacing all its exchange equipment with this new electronic equipment to speed communications and provide new services. Speech and data can be connected by this new system. Customers can be connected to advanced network services such as e-mail or fax.

Telcommunciation

Transmitting and receiving information electronically or electrically by means of coaxial cables, broadcast radio or telephone lines between two or more terminals.

Teleconferencing

A way to hold meetings by phone. You can use your own phone. BT links a number of callers by dialling out or individuals can join the conference by dialling in. Teleconferencing has to be arranged through BT's Conference Call Bureau.

Telecopier

Device for transmitting documents by telephone where both the sender and recipient have machines which can copy documents and transmit and receive them. The receiving machine reproduces the documents.

Telephone

An instrument with a microphone and receiver mounted on a handset for transmitting speech. Also the means of communication using such instruments. Users can hire or buy phones. They are charged a quarterly rental fee for use of the phone lines and any phones they have hired. Phone calls are charged by the time spent on the call by units. Phones can be combined with answering machines and faxes.

Telephone answering machine interface

A device to enable you to connect your answering machine to your fax machine.

Teleprinter

A machine with a typewriter keyboard used to send and receive telegraph messages, which is now done almost entirely by electrical impulses. The message stays on the machine until it is wanted and is then printed onto a roll of paper. It automatically records transmission and receipt details and automatically redials if the line is engaged.

Telex

An international communication service whereby users hire teleprinters to transfer messages. The main service in Britain is BT's Telex.

It is also used to describe a teleprinter used in this way. Although being superseded by fax machines, 1.7 million people use the system worldwide.

The system consists of automatic printers which are interconnected between terminals over a dedicated network. Each terminal has an individual number and can identify other terminals by means of an answer-back code. A message can be typed on one printer and it is printed simultaneously on the receiving printer. This means that operators can have 'conversations' and both questions and answers are recorded identically on both printers for both parties. The system can be left open to receive messages at night.

Electronic teleprinters allow Telex messages to be stored and sent automatically and will redial the number if it is engaged.

Modern teleprinters have a VDU (Visual Display Unit) on which the operator can type and receive messages while the teleprinter receives and sends messages.

173

Thermal paper

Paper for fax machines which can be printed on by means of heat.

Three-way calling

The ability to set up a three-way conversation between one person on an outside line and two on internal extensions.

Trunk offering

An internal telephone operator or switchboard operator can signal that they wish to interrupt a call. They can do this by pressing a button which causes a series of high pitched bleeps to sound on the line.

Unattended night calls

Bells are placed around the building. When an incoming call is made all the bells ring. Anyone who hears a bell picks up the nearest phone, dials '8', and receives the call.

VDU (visual display unit)

A computer or adapted television screen which can display data.

Videoconferencing

This is a means of seeing and talking to people who are in another place. Videoconferencing takes place either in one of BT's public videoconferencing centres or the equipment can be installed in your office. Communication is by means of video and phone equipment in each centre.

Videophone

A phone with a small screen which lifts up. If the recipient also has a videophone you can see a colour picture of the caller as well as talk to them. The phone can either be used as a 'voice only' phone or can provide a colour image on the two connecting units. It can also show a still close-up shot.

Videotex

An electronic system which enables computer based information to be made available via a visual display unit (VDU) or adapted television set.

Viewdata

Database which is accessed via remote terminals. Public systems use phone lines.

X-stream

A special network of private lines. Four types give voice or data transmission including offering a satellite link.

Appendix 1
Telephone training

■

BT is the principal organisation which provides training in the use of its modern communications equipment as well as training in telephone responses.

There are three or four main commercial outfits which sell telephone training programmes but most of these are situated in South East England. Your local Chamber of Commerce can supply the names of other companies in your local area who can provide training.

BT can provide training at three residential centres, at a number of national centres or your company site. Information about Customer Training courses and up to date information on prices can be obtained by phoning BT Customer Training on 0800 585 775, or write to BT Customer Training, Redwing House, Kents Hill Training Centre, H8 Standing Way, Milton Keynes, MK7 6TT. Terms for on-site training will be negotiated. Courses include the following:

Educational Portfolio

First Steps In Data Communications (1 day, non-residential, London)

Data Transmission Appreciation (2 days, non-residential, London)

Digital Appreciation (2 days, non-residential, London)

First Steps In Packet Switching (1 day, non-residential, London)

Packet Switching Principles (2 days, non-residential, London)

X25 Applications (4 days, non-residential, London)

Integrated Digital Network Course (3 days, residential, Bournemouth)

Data Communications Foundation Course (3 days, residential in Bournemouth or non-residential, London)

Introduction to Data Communications for Technical Managers (5 days, residential, Stone)

Voice Communications – Foundation Course (5 days, residential in Bournemouth or non-residential, London)

Technical Portfolio

Meridian 1 System Administrators Course (5 days, residential, Bournemouth)

Meridian 1 ACD Course (3 days, residential, Bournemouth)

Meridian MAX Course (7 days, residential, Bournemouth)

BT iSDX System Managers Course (4 days, residential, Bournemouth)

BTeX System Managers Course (5 days, residential, Bournemouth)

BTeX ACD System Managers Course, Parts 1 and 2, Bournemouth (7 days, residential)

T-NET GP Local Area Network System Managers Course (5 days, residential, Bournemouth)

T-NET PC Local Area Network System Managers Course (4 days, residential, Bournemouth)

Communications as a Business Tool

Telephone Techniques (1 day, non-residential, national centres)

Collection of overdue accounts (1 day, non-residential, national centres)

Telemarketing (3 days, residential, Bournemouth)

Telesales (2 days)

<u>176</u> BT has national centres at Aberdeen, Belfast, Birmingham, Bracknell, Brighton, Bristol, Cambridge, Canterbury, Colchester, Ealing, Edinburgh, Glasgow, Harrow, Leeds, Leicester, Manchester, Milton Keynes, Newcastle, Norwich, Nottingham, Oxford, Plymouth, Portsmouth, Preston, Sheffield, Southend-on-Sea, Southampton, and Worthing.

Appendix 2
Addresses

■

BT: British Telecommunications plc
Registered Office: 81 Newgate Street, London EC1A 7AJ General correspond-
ence to BT, Freepost BS6295, Bristol BS1 2BR

BT Customer Training
Redwing House, Kents Hill Training Centre, H8 Standing Way, Milton Keynes
MK7 6TT Tel: 0800 585 775 Fax: 0908 356715

BT Order Direct
Freepost (BS7632), Bristol, BS1 2QX Tel: 0800 800 150

Call Connections
No 1 Brunel Way, Slough SL1 1XL

Cellnet
No 1 Brunel Way, Slough, SL1 1XL

Cellnet Sales Hire Service
32 Shoreditch High Street, London E1 Tel: 071-247 0101

Cellphone Group plc
The Cellphone House, North Circular Road, London NW10 Tel: 081-961 7000

DTI: Department of Trade and Industry
Ashdown House, Victoria Street, DTI: General Enquiries, London SW1 Tel:
071-215 5000

Hutchison Telecom
(Rabbit phone suppliers) Rabbit Information Service, Freepost (SW5198),
London SW6 1YY Tel: 0800 286 286

Mercury Communications Limited
Registered Office: New Mercury House, 26 Red Lion Square, London WC1R
4HQ Tel: 071-528 2000

Metropolitan Police
New Scotland Yard, Broadway, London SW1H OBG Tel: 071-230 1212 Fax:
071-230 4276

Office of Telecommunications (OFTEL)
Export House, 50 Ludgate Hill, London EC4M 7JJ Tel: 071-634 8700

Telecommunications and Posts Division, DTI
Kingsgate House, 66–74 Victoria Street, London SW1 6SW Tel: 071-215 5000

Telecommunications Managers Association
40 Chatsworth Parade, Petts Wood Tel: Orpington 31633

Telecommunications Users Association
48 Percy Road, London N12 8BU Tel: 081-445 0996

Teleconomy
6 Southampton Place, London WC1A 2DA

Vodafone
32 Shoreditch High Street, London E1 Tel: 071-247 0101

Appendix 3
Bibliography

■

Cochrane, Pat. (1993). *The Power of the Phone*, Pitman.

Foster, Thelma J. (1985). *Telephone and Reception Skills*, Stanley Thorne (Publishers) Ltd.

Harrison, John. (1992). *Secretarial Duties*, Pitman.

King, Elizabeth. (1987). *Office Technology Terms*, Pitman.

Lewis, David. (1991). *Be Your Own Boss*, British Telcommunications plc.

Lewis, David, and Fielding, Guy. (1991). *The Language of Success*, British Telecommunications plc.

Lloyd, Sam R. (1988). *How to Develop Assertiveness*, Kogan Page.

Martindale, Ruth. (1988). *Office Procedures*, Chambers Commerce Series.

Mills, Geoffrey, and Standingford, Oliver, and Appleby, Robert C. (1991). *Modern Office Management*, Pitman.

Montcrieff, Joan, and Sharp, Doreen. (1980). *The Professional Secretary's Handbook*, Papermac.

Paisley, Brenda and Parker. (1983). *Thank You for Calling – Telephone and Reception Skills*, Pitman.

Stubbs, David R. (1985). *Assertiveness at Work*, Pan.

Treacy, Declan. (1991). *Clear Your Desk!*, Century Business.

Index

■

183